Pathways to Passive Profits

Launching Your Affiliate Marketing Journey: Understanding Strategies, Building Trust, and Navigating the Digital Marketplace for Newbies

Ethan Sinclair

Summary

Chapter 1: Introduction to Affiliate Marketing................................5

The Essence of Passive Profits 9

Unveiling Affiliate Marketing..14

Evolution of Digital Marketing Landscape 20

The Promise of Affiliate Marketing for Newbies 25

Chapter 2: Understanding Affiliate Marketing Strategies........... 31

Decoding Affiliate Marketing Channels 36

Unleashing the Power of Content Marketing 42

The Role of Social Media in Affiliate Success........................46

Exploring Paid Advertising for Affiliates 50

Chapter 3: Building Trust and Credibility as an Affiliate Marketer **56**

The Trust Factor in Affiliate Marketing................................61

Crafting High-Quality and Trustworthy Content....................66

Nurturing Authentic Relationships with Your Audience 71

Utilizing Transparency to Strengthen Credibility..................75

Chapter 4: Navigating the Digital Marketplace for Affiliate Success.. **80**

Choosing the Right Affiliate Products or Services...................84

Researching Your Niche and Target Audience 89

The Art of Effective Market Positioning.................................93

Leveraging Analytics to Optimize Your Strategy....................98

Chapter 5: Establishing Your Affiliate Marketing Platform......**104**

Creating a Professional and Engaging Website or Blog.................. 110

Search Engine Optimization (SEO) for Visibility and Traffic........ 114

Chapter 6: Maximizing Affiliate Earnings and Scaling Up.........**120**

Beyond Beginners: Scaling Your Affiliate Business 125

Exploring Advanced Affiliate Marketing Techniques 130

Automated Tools and Their Role in Passive Income 134

The Future Landscape of Affiliate Marketing 138

Chapter 7: Overcoming Challenges and Staying Resilient 142

Common Pitfalls to Avoid in Affiliate Marketing 146

Navigating Fluctuations in the Digital Market 151

Compliance, Ethics, and Longevity in Affiliate Marketing 155

Chapter 1: Introduction to Affiliate Marketing

In today's digital era, the world of business and marketing has undergone a significant transformation. Traditional advertising methods are gradually being overshadowed by novel and more effective strategies. One such marketing technique that has gained immense popularity and proven to be a game-changer is affiliate marketing. This chapter serves as an introduction to this powerful marketing concept, shedding light on its history, benefits, and core principles.

Origin and Evolution:

Affiliate marketing traces its roots back to the mid-1990s when the concept was pioneered by William J. Tobin, the founder of PC Flowers & Gifts. Tobin recognized the potential of leveraging existing networks and websites to promote products and devised an innovative payment scheme based on performance. This idea revolutionized the marketing landscape by introducing a cost-effective method to reach a vast audience.

Over the years, affiliate marketing has evolved and matured into a sophisticated ecosystem, capturing a significant portion of online advertising revenue. The advent of search engines and e-commerce platforms provided a fertile ground for affiliate marketers to thrive. Today, it is estimated that the affiliate marketing industry contributes billions of dollars to the global economy annually.

Understanding Affiliate Marketing:

In essence, affiliate marketing refers to a partnership between a business (known as the merchant or advertiser) and independent individuals or entities (known as affiliates or publishers). The main objective of this collaboration is to drive traffic, generate leads, or facilitate direct sales for the merchant, in exchange for a commission.

Affiliates employ various techniques to promote the merchant's products or services. These may include utilizing websites, blogs, social media platforms, email marketing, search engine optimization, paid advertising, or other creative methods tailored to their target audience. When a customer purchases a product or performs a specific action, such as filling out a form or clicking on an advertisement, the affiliate receives a predetermined commission, ensuring a win-win arrangement for both parties.

Benefits of Affiliate Marketing:

1. Cost-effective: Unlike traditional marketing channels that bear a high upfront cost, affiliate marketing is performance-based. Merchants pay affiliates only when desired outcomes are achieved, such as a sale or lead, making it an economical option for businesses

of all sizes.

2. Expanded reach: Affiliates act as brand ambassadors, extending the merchant's reach to untapped markets and diverse audiences. This vast network can expose products or services to a wider customer base, resulting in increased visibility and potential sales.

3. Minimal risk: Affiliate marketing mitigates the risk commonly associated with traditional advertising campaigns. Merchants only pay commissions upon successful conversions, reducing the likelihood of wasting resources on ineffective marketing efforts.

4. Enhanced credibility: Leveraging the trust and reputation of affiliates enhances the merchant's credibility. Consumers are more likely to make a purchase when recommended by a trustworthy source, leading to increased conversions and customer loyalty.

5. Scalability and flexibility: Affiliate marketing enables businesses to scale their marketing efforts seamlessly. By partnering with multiple affiliates, merchants can widen their presence and adapt campaigns based on market trends and consumer preferences.

Core Principles of Affiliate Marketing:

1. Choosing the right affiliates: An essential step in launching a successful affiliate marketing campaign is selecting suitable partners. It is crucial to assess their industry expertise, target audience

alignment, online presence, and marketing approach. Developing strong relationships with affiliates ensures a shared vision and mutual success.

2. Tracking and measurement: Precise tracking and analytics are fundamental to assess the effectiveness of affiliate marketing campaigns. Businesses should implement robust monitoring systems to accurately measure conversions, sales, traffic, and other key performance indicators (KPIs). These insights enable optimizing strategies and maximizing return on investment (ROI).

3. Compelling content creation: High-quality content is at the heart of successful affiliate marketing. Affiliates need to engage their audience with captivating and highly relevant content, showcasing the value and benefits of the merchant's products or services. Effective content creation fosters consumer trust and drives conversions.

4. Compliance and transparency: Adhering to ethical practices, industry regulations, and legal requirements is paramount for both merchants and affiliates. Transparency regarding promotional activities, affiliations, and disclosures builds trust and credibility among consumers. Non-compliance can severely damage reputations and expose businesses to legal consequences.

The Essence of Passive Profits

In the vast landscape of financial independence, the concept of generating passive profits has garnered widespread admiration and intrigue. Many individuals fantasize about a life where money flows effortlessly, allowing them to enjoy the finer things without continuous toil. Contrary to popular belief, attaining passive profits is not an inaccessible dream but a realistic goal with the right knowledge, strategies, and a disciplined approach. In this chapter, we will delve into the essence of passive profits, understanding its intricacies, and discovering the multitude of avenues to achieve this coveted financial freedom.

Section 1: Understanding Passive Profit

1.1 Defining Passive Profits:

To embark on a journey towards passive profits, it is crucial to comprehend its core essence. Passive profits refer to the income generated without active involvement or direct exchange of time for money. Unlike active income, where individuals trade their time and efforts, passive profits allow for a continuous stream of revenue with minimal effort once the initial work is executed. The key lies in leveraging assets, systems, or investments that generate income independently over time.

1.2 The Power of Passive Profits:

The allure of passive profits lies in its potential to provide financial stability, freedom, and the ability to break free from the constraints of traditional employment. By generating income passively, individuals open doors to more fulfilling pursuits, such as pursuing hobbies, spending quality time with loved ones, or exploring new business ventures. Moreover, passive profits act as a safety net, ensuring a consistent income stream even during economic downturns or unforeseen circumstances.

Section 2: Unveiling the Avenues

2.1 Rental Properties:

Real estate investment has proven to be a reliable and time-tested path to passive profits. By owning rental properties, individuals can generate a steady stream of income through monthly rent payments. With careful property selection, proactive tenant management, and smart financing strategies, rental properties can become a lucrative vehicle for passive profits.

2.2 Dividend Investing:

Dividend investing involves purchasing shares of companies that distribute a portion of their profits to shareholders in the form of dividends. By selecting dividend-paying stocks, investors can create a portfolio that generates regular cash flows, allowing for passive profits to grow over time. This method requires a deep understanding of the stock market, careful stock selection, and patience to reap the rewards of compounding dividends.

2.3 E-commerce and Online Businesses:

The rise of the digital age has unlocked unprecedented opportunities for passive profits through e-commerce and online businesses. Platforms like Amazon, Shopify, or eBay enable entrepreneurs to create online stores, sell products, and automate processes such as inventory management and shipping. Embracing digital marketing techniques and building a brand presence can amplify the passive profit potential of these ventures.

2.4 Intellectual Property:

Entrepreneurs, authors, musicians, and creative minds can monetize their intellectual property to achieve passive profits. Creating and selling e-books, licensing music, selling courses, or generating income from patents and inventions are all viable paths towards sustaining passive income. Leveraging digital platforms and emerging technologies can significantly enhance exposure to potential customers while minimizing the effort required for ongoing revenue generation.

2.5 Peer-to-Peer Lending:

The emergence of peer-to-peer lending platforms presents an alternative to traditional banking systems by connecting borrowers directly with lenders. By carefully assessing the risks and adjusting for diversification, investors can lend money to individuals or small businesses and earn interest on those loans. With the right strategy and proper risk management, peer-to-peer lending can be an effective avenue to generate passive profits.

Section 3: Strategies for Passive Profit Success

3.1 Setting Realistic Goals:

Before embarking on any passive profit venture, it is crucial to set realistic and measurable goals. Identifying the desired level of income, defining a timeline, and understanding the resources required will determine the most suitable avenue to pursue. By clarifying objectives, individuals can focus their efforts and devise effective strategies accordingly.

3.2 Leveraging Technology:

Technology plays a pivotal role in achieving passive profits. Automation tools, online platforms, and digital marketing techniques enable entrepreneurs to streamline processes, minimize manual labor, and reach a global audience effortlessly. Embracing technology can significantly increase passive profit potential while reducing ongoing effort and costs.

3.3 Diversification:

Relying on a single passive profit avenue can be risky. Diversification across multiple streams mitigates the potential impact of economic fluctuations, market shifts, or individual investment risks. Allocating resources across various asset classes or business ventures allows individuals to create a resilient and sustainable passive profit portfolio.

3.4 Continuous Learning and Adaptation:
The landscape of passive profits is ever-evolving; it is crucial to stay
abreast of new opportunities, emerging trends, and best practices.
Cultivating a habit of continuous learning, attending seminars,
reading industry publications, and networking with like-minded
individuals can help individuals adapt to changing market dynamics
and optimize their passive profit strategy.

While this chapter has explored the essence of passive profits, it is
only the beginning of an in-depth journey towards achieving
financial independence. Understanding the definition, exploring
different avenues, and adopting the right strategies are just stepping
stones in a vast realm of possibilities. By embracing a proactive
mindset, relentless pursuit of knowledge, and disciplined execution,
anyone can unlock the potential of passive profits and embark on a
path towards a fulfilling and abundant future.

Unveiling Affiliate Marketing

Affiliate marketing has emerged as one of the most lucrative and effective ways to generate income online. It has revolutionized the way businesses promote their products and services while providing individuals with opportunities to earn passive income. In this chapter, we will delve deeper into the world of affiliate marketing, unraveling its purpose, benefits, techniques, and potential hurdles. Whether you are a business looking to expand your reach or an aspiring affiliate marketer seeking financial freedom, this chapter will serve as your comprehensive guide to understanding and mastering the art of affiliate marketing.

Understanding Affiliate Marketing

At its core, affiliate marketing is a performance-based marketing strategy where individuals, commonly referred to as affiliates, partner with businesses to promote their products or services. Affiliates earn a commission for each customer they refer to the business through their unique affiliate link. These links, often embedded in URLs or banners, redirect potential customers to the business's website or landing page.

The process of affiliate marketing begins when an affiliate agrees to promote a product or service. They typically choose products that align with their niche or target audience to ensure that their marketing efforts are highly targeted and effective. Once an affiliate has selected the products they wish to promote, they receive a unique affiliate link. This link is the key to tracking the traffic and sales generated by the affiliate, enabling accurate commission calculations.

Advantages of Affiliate Marketing

Affiliate marketing offers numerous advantages for both businesses and affiliates, making it an attractive option for generating income. Let's take a closer look at some of these advantages:

1. Low Investment: One of the greatest benefits of affiliate marketing is that it requires minimal upfront investment. Affiliates do not need to develop their own products or services, manage inventory, or handle customer support. This significantly reduces the financial risks associated with starting an online business.

2. Passive Income: Affiliate marketing allows individuals to generate passive income streams. Once an affiliate has set up their marketing campaigns and established a steady flow of traffic, they can earn commissions even while sleeping or enjoying leisure time. This gives affiliates the freedom to focus on other ventures or simply enjoy their newfound financial freedom.

3. Wide Range of Products: As an affiliate marketer, one is not limited to promoting a single product or brand. There is a vast array

of products and services available in every industry, providing affiliates with endless options. This flexibility allows affiliates to explore different niches and diversify their income streams.

4. Scalability: Unlike traditional businesses, affiliate marketing has virtually no scalability limitations. Affiliates can expand their reach, increase their audience, and promote multiple products simultaneously without the burden of physical infrastructure or additional staff. This scalability potential allows affiliates to maximize their earning potential.

5. Cost-Effective Marketing: For businesses, affiliate marketing offers a cost-effective advertising solution. Instead of relying solely on expensive marketing campaigns or paid advertisements, businesses can leverage the influential power of affiliates to reach a broader audience at a fraction of the cost.

Understanding the Affiliate Marketing Process

To succeed as an affiliate marketer, it is essential to grasp the various steps involved in the affiliate marketing process. Let's break it down:

1. Research and Select a Niche: The first step in affiliate marketing is to identify and select a niche. A niche represents a specialized segment within an industry. It is crucial to choose a niche that matches your interests, expertise, and target audience. This ensures that your marketing efforts are effective and resonate with your

audience.

2. Identify Profitable Affiliate Programs: Once you have selected a niche, the next step is to research and identify profitable affiliate programs. Consider factors such as commission rates, cookie durations, conversion rates, payment structures, and the reputation of the affiliate programs. Partnering with reputable and high-paying affiliate programs enhances your chances of earning substantial commissions.

3. Build a Website or Blog: Your website or blog serves as the primary platform for your affiliate marketing activities. Create a user-friendly, visually appealing website with valuable content that attracts and engages your target audience. Incorporate your affiliate links strategically within your content to increase conversion rates.

4. Drive Targeted Traffic: Traffic is the lifeblood of any affiliate marketing campaign. Implement various strategies like search engine optimization (SEO), social media marketing, content marketing, and email marketing to drive targeted traffic to your website. The quality and relevance of the traffic play a significant role in determining your conversion rates and overall success.

5. Promote Affiliate Products: Now that you have set the stage, it's time to promote affiliate products. This can be done through various forms of content such as product reviews, comparisons, buyer's guides, or by sharing personal experiences and testimonials.

Integrate your affiliate links seamlessly within your content, making it easy for your audience to make a purchase.

6. Track and Optimize: Constantly monitor and analyze the performance of your affiliate marketing campaigns. Track your clicks, conversions, sales, and commission earnings to identify areas that require improvement. Optimize your campaigns by refining your content, testing new strategies, and staying updated with the latest industry trends.

Challenges in Affiliate Marketing

While affiliate marketing presents countless opportunities, it also comes with its fair share of challenges. Acknowledging and addressing these challenges ahead of time are key to long-term success. Let's explore some common hurdles faced by affiliate marketers:

1. Intense Competition: The barrier to entry in affiliate marketing is relatively low, resulting in a saturated market. The intense competition can make it difficult to stand out from the crowd and gain traction. To overcome this challenge, focus on innovation, developing a unique selling proposition, and consistently providing value to your target audience.

2. Building Trust: As an affiliate marketer, establishing trust with your audience is essential for driving conversions. Many potential

customers may be skeptical due to previous negative experiences with misleading or spammy affiliate marketing campaigns. To build trust, provide honest and unbiased reviews, be transparent about your affiliate relationships, and only promote high-quality products or services.

3. SEO Competition: Search engine optimization is crucial for organic traffic generation. However, ranking high in search engine results pages can be challenging due to intense SEO competition. To improve your chances of ranking, conduct thorough keyword research, create high-quality and optimized content, build quality backlinks, and stay updated with SEO best practices.

4. Adapting to Industry Changes: The affiliate marketing landscape is constantly evolving. Affiliate marketers must be adaptable and willing to learn new strategies and platforms as technology advances. Staying informed about industry trends and changes will help you remain competitive and ensure long-term success.

In this chapter, we've uncovered the true essence of affiliate marketing, exploring its purpose, benefits, techniques, and potential challenges. Affiliate marketing signifies a remarkable opportunity for businesses to expand their reach and for individuals to generate passive income. By understanding the affiliate marketing process, leveraging its advantages, and proactively addressing challenges, you can embark on a profitable journey and achieve financial freedom in the vast realm of affiliate marketing.

Evolution of Digital Marketing Landscape

In this digital age, the marketing landscape has undergone a tremendous transformation. The advent of the internet and the emergence of new technologies have revolutionized how businesses interact with consumers. In this chapter, we will delve into the evolution of the digital marketing landscape, exploring its various stages and analyzing the key factors that have shaped its trajectory. From the early days of the internet to the era of social media dominance, we will trace the significant milestones that have propelled digital marketing to its current state. So, sit back, relax, and embark on a journey through the ever-evolving world of digital marketing.

1. The Birth of the Internet: The Dawn of a New Era

It all began with the birth of the internet. In the late 1960s, a network called ARPANET was created, connecting computers across different locations. However, it was not until the 1990s that the internet started gaining widespread popularity. With the advent of Web 1.0, the static nature of websites and limited user interaction posed significant challenges for marketers. Traditional marketing methods such as print, broadcast, and outdoor advertising continued to dominate, while the true potential of digital marketing lay dormant, waiting to be unleashed.

2. The Rise of E-Commerce: A Game-Changer for Businesses

As the internet gained momentum, a new concept emerged: e-commerce. Electronic commerce offered businesses an opportunity to expand their reach beyond physical storefronts and tap into the global market. For the first time, businesses could sell their products and services directly to consumers online, eliminating the need for intermediaries. Companies like Amazon and eBay became pioneers in this space, shaping the digital marketing landscape of the late 1990s and early 2000s. Marketers swiftly realized the untapped potential of digital platforms and began exploring ways to leverage them for promotional purposes.

3. Search Engines: The Gateway to the Digital Universe

Search engines revolutionized how information was discovered on the internet, and consequently, the way marketers approached digital advertising. The rise of search engines like Yahoo, AltaVista, and ultimately, Google, paved the way for search engine marketing (SEM) and search engine optimization (SEO). Marketers now had a new avenue to showcase their products and services directly to users who were actively searching for them. Keywords and content relevancy became crucial factors in optimizing websites to appear prominently in search engine results pages (SERPs).

4. Social Media: The Power of Connection

The mid-2000s witnessed the rise of social media platforms that fundamentally transformed the digital marketing landscape.

Websites like MySpace and Friendster brought people closer than ever before, enabling them to connect, share, and express themselves online. Facebook, founded in 2004, emerged as a game-changer, offering advertisers an unprecedented opportunity to target specific demographics and personalize their marketing campaigns. Brands quickly recognized the potential of social media marketing (SMM) and began allocating substantial resources to gain visibility and engage with their target audience directly.

5. Mobile Revolution: On-the-Go Marketing

The widespread adoption of smartphones in the late 2000s became a game-changer for digital marketing. With more people accessing the internet through mobile devices, marketers had to adapt their strategies to engage users on-the-go. Mobile marketing, including mobile advertising and mobile app marketing, gained prominence as a necessity rather than an option. Location-based targeting and personalized push notifications opened up new avenues for businesses to reach consumers at the right time and in the right place. Mobile apps became an integral part of brand communication and customer engagement.

6. Content Marketing: Engaging and Informative

As the digital marketing landscape evolved, consumers became increasingly adept at filtering out promotional messages. This shift in consumer behavior led to the rise of content marketing as a crucial strategy for businesses. Rather than bombarding users with aggressive advertising, brands began focusing on creating valuable, informative, and engaging content tailored to their target audience. Blogging, video marketing, and influencer collaborations flourished, establishing credibility and building long-term relationships with consumers. The emphasis shifted from the hard sell to providing value and building trust.

7. Inbound Marketing: Customer-Centric Approach

The advent of content marketing paved the way for a broader concept - inbound marketing. Inbound marketing focuses on attracting and engaging customers through relevant content, rather than interruptive advertising. It encompasses various strategies such as content creation, social media marketing, search engine optimization, email marketing, and more. Inbound marketing recognizes the power of building relationships with customers and creating a seamless user experience across different digital touchpoints. By providing valuable insights and addressing customer pain points, businesses can attract, convert, and retain customers more effectively.

8. Personalization: The Age of Individualized Marketing

With the wealth of data available in the digital realm, marketers began to realize the power of personalization. By leveraging customer data, behavior tracking, and advanced analytics, businesses could deliver highly tailored marketing messages to individual consumers. Personalization allows marketers to create relevant and timely experiences, ultimately increasing engagement and conversion rates. Whether through email marketing, website customization, or social media advertising, personalization has become a central aspect of digital marketing, empowering businesses to provide unique experiences for each customer.

9. Artificial Intelligence: Augmenting Marketing Abilities

As we step into the future, artificial intelligence (AI) is reshaping the digital marketing landscape once again. AI-powered technologies like machine learning and natural language processing enable marketers to analyze vast amounts of data, gain valuable insights, and automate various marketing processes. Chatbots, for instance, deliver personalized customer support, while predictive analytics helps businesses forecast buying patterns and identify opportunities for growth. AI enhances digital marketing capabilities, providing businesses with a competitive edge in an increasingly data-driven era.

The digital marketing landscape has transformed significantly over the years, evolving from static websites and limited user interaction to a dynamic, personalized, and engaging environment. From the birth of the internet to the rise of e-commerce, the dominance of search engines, social media's power of connection, mobile revolution, content marketing, inbound marketing, personalization, and the advent of AI, the journey has been nothing short of incredible. The digital marketing landscape will continue to evolve, driven by technological advancements and changing consumer behaviors. As marketers, it is our duty to adapt, stay agile, and embrace the opportunities that lie ahead in this ever-evolving digital world.

The Promise of Affiliate Marketing for Newbies

Affiliate marketing has emerged as a lucrative career opportunity for individuals seeking financial independence and the flexibility to work on their own terms. With the digital landscape evolving at a rapid pace, the world of affiliate marketing has opened up a world of possibilities for newbies wanting to carve a niche for themselves in the online business realm.

In this chapter, we will delve into the promise of affiliate marketing for newbies, exploring how this industry operates, its potential benefits, and the steps you can take to jumpstart your affiliate marketing journey.

1. Understanding Affiliate Marketing

Before we explore the promise of affiliate marketing, it is imperative to have a clear understanding of what it entails. At its core, affiliate marketing is a performance-based marketing strategy that allows individuals, known as affiliates, to earn commissions by promoting other people's or businesses' products or services. Affiliates earn a commission every time a sale is made through their unique affiliate links.

This unique business model sets affiliate marketing apart from traditional marketing techniques, as it allows individuals to only focus on promoting, leaving the complexities of inventory management, customer support, and product delivery to the merchants or business owners.

2. The Promise of Affiliate Marketing

2.1. Minimal Startup Costs

One of the primary promises of affiliate marketing is the low barrier to entry. Unlike starting a traditional brick-and-mortar business, affiliate marketing requires minimal upfront investment. All you need is a computer, internet access, and the willingness to learn and put in the effort to succeed. This opens up a world of opportunities for newbies with limited resources to break into the online entrepreneurial sphere.

2.2. Unlimited Income Potential

Another enticing aspect of affiliate marketing is its unlimited income potential. As an affiliate, your earnings are not capped by a fixed salary or hourly wage. Instead, your income is determined by your ability to drive traffic, generate leads, and convert those leads into sales. This means that the harder you work and the more successful you become, the greater your earning potential. Many affiliate marketers have managed to build sustainable, full-time incomes, allowing them to live life on their own terms.

2.3. Flexibility and Freedom

Affiliate marketing offers a level of flexibility and freedom that is rarely found in traditional employment opportunities. As an affiliate, you have the freedom to choose the products or services you want to promote, the platforms you wish to utilize, and the work schedule that suits you best. This allows you to create a perfect work-life balance and take control of your own destiny. Whether you prefer working from the comfort of your home or want to travel and work remotely, affiliate marketing offers you the freedom to shape your career around your ideal lifestyle.

2.4. Passive Income Potential

One of the most exciting promises of affiliate marketing is the potential to generate passive income. Unlike traditional jobs where you exchange your time for money, affiliate marketing allows you to earn money even while you sleep. Once you have set up your affiliate links and built a strong foundation, your promotional efforts can continue to generate income for you on autopilot. Of course, it requires consistent effort and dedication to reach a point where passive income becomes a reality, but the promise of earning money while you're not actively working is undoubtedly appealing.

3. Getting Started in Affiliate Marketing

Now that we have explored the promise of affiliate marketing, let us delve into the crucial steps you need to take as a newbie to jumpstart your affiliate marketing journey:

3.1. Identify Your Niche

Before you venture into the world of affiliate marketing, it is crucial to identify your niche – a specific area or industry that aligns with your interests and expertise. By narrowing down your focus, you can tailor your promotional efforts to a specific target audience, increasing your chances of success. Take the time to research different niches, analyze market trends, and evaluate your own passions and knowledge base to identify a niche that offers both profitability and personal fulfillment.

3.2. Choose Reliable Affiliate Programs

Once you have identified your niche, the next step is to find reliable affiliate programs that offer products or services related to your chosen niche. Look for programs that provide competitive commissions, valuable resources for affiliates, and a reputable track record. Popular affiliate networks such as Amazon Associates, ClickBank, and Commission Junction offer a vast array of products and services across various industries, making them excellent starting points for newbies.

3.3. Build Your Online Presence

To thrive in affiliate marketing, you need a strong online presence. Start by creating a website or blog that serves as the foundation for your promotional efforts. Optimize your website for search engines, publish high-quality content, and focus on building a loyal audience. Additionally, leverage social media platforms to expand your reach and engage with potential customers. Remember, your online presence acts as a gateway to your affiliate promotions, so invest time and effort into creating an appealing and trustworthy brand.

3.4. Create Valuable Content

Content is king in the world of affiliate marketing. Producing high-quality, valuable content is crucial for establishing yourself as an authority in your niche, attracting organic traffic, and driving conversions. Whether you choose to write detailed blog posts, create video tutorials, or record informative podcasts, focus on delivering content that educates, entertains, and solves problems for your target audience. The more value you offer, the more likely your audience will trust your recommendations and make purchases through your affiliate links.

3.5. Nurture Relationships and Promote Ethically

Successful affiliate marketing relies on building trust with your audience. Instead of bombarding them with endless promotional content, strive to nurture authentic relationships with your followers. Engage with your audience, answer their questions, and provide valuable insights. By positioning yourself as a trusted advisor, you increase the chances that your audience will purchase products or services based on your recommendations. Be ethical in your promotions, disclose your affiliate partnerships, and only endorse products you genuinely believe in. Trust and integrity are paramount for long-term success in the affiliate marketing industry.

In The promise of affiliate marketing for newbies is indeed enticing. With its minimal startup costs, unlimited income potential, flexibility, and passive income opportunities, affiliate marketing opens doors for individuals looking to break free from the constraints of traditional employment.

However, it is important to remember that success in affiliate marketing requires dedication, continuous learning, and patience. Embrace the journey, stay curious, adapt to changes in the industry, and remember that building a sustainable affiliate marketing empire takes time and effort.

So, go ahead, dive into the world of affiliate marketing, armed with the knowledge and understanding of the immense promise it holds for aspiring newbies like yourself.

Remember, the journey is yours to explore and the possibilities are endless.

Chapter 2: Understanding Affiliate Marketing Strategies

Welcome to Chapter 2 of our comprehensive guide on affiliate marketing strategies. In this chapter, we will delve deeper into the world of affiliate marketing and explore various effective strategies that can help you maximize your earnings and achieve success in this competitive industry. Understanding these strategies is crucial for anyone seeking to build a profitable affiliate marketing business. So, let's dive right in!

1. Choosing the Right Affiliate Program:

One of the primary steps in affiliate marketing is selecting the right program to promote. It's vital to choose a program that aligns with your niche, interests, and target audience. Consider factors such as commission rates, product quality, brand reputation, and conversion rates when making your decision. Conduct thorough research and evaluate different programs to find the one that best suits your needs and preferences.

2. Utilizing Quality Content:

In affiliate marketing, content is king. Creating high-quality, engaging content is essential to attract and retain your target audience.

Whether it's a blog post, video, social media content, or an email newsletter, focus on providing value to your audience and promoting products or services in a genuine and informative manner. Utilize SEO techniques to optimize your content for search engines and increase your visibility to potential customers.

3. Building an Engaged Audience:

To succeed in affiliate marketing, you must have an engaged and loyal audience. Building a strong relationship with your audience takes time and effort. Interact with your audience through comments, messages, and social media platforms. Aim to provide solutions to their problems and answer their questions promptly. By becoming a trusted source of valuable information, you'll increase your chances of earning their trust and converting them into paying customers.

4. Diversifying Promotional Channels:

Relying solely on one promotional channel can limit your reach and potential earnings. To maximize your exposure and attract a wider audience, leverage multiple channels such as social media, blogging, email marketing, and YouTube. Each channel has its unique advantages, so diversify your efforts to tap into different demographics and expand your affiliate marketing business.

5. Harnessing the Power of Email Marketing:

Email marketing remains one of the most effective strategies for affiliate marketers. It allows you to nurture relationships with your subscribers and promote products or services directly to their inbox. By offering valuable content and exclusive offers, you can build trust and credibility, increasing the likelihood of conversions. Craft compelling email campaigns, segment your audience, and track your metrics to optimize your email marketing strategy.

6. Capitalizing on Influencer Marketing:

Influencer marketing has gained significant momentum in recent years and can be a powerful tool for affiliate marketers. Collaborating with influencers in your niche can expose your affiliate products to their dedicated and engaged followers. When choosing influencers, consider their relevancy, credibility, and engagement rate. Ensure that their brand aligns with yours to maintain authenticity and maximize your chances of success.

7. Leveraging Social Media:

Social media platforms such as Facebook, Instagram, Twitter, and TikTok provide immense opportunities for affiliates to connect with their target audience. Create engaging and shareable content, run targeted ad campaigns, and actively engage with your followers to build a strong social media presence. Leverage social media analytics to identify which platforms and content formats generate the most engagement and conversions.

8. Implementing Search Engine Optimization (SEO):

Search engine optimization is crucial for driving organic traffic to your website or blog. Conduct keyword research and optimize your content with relevant keywords to improve your website's visibility on search engine results pages (SERPs). Quality backlinks, proper site structure, and mobile-friendly design are also important aspects of SEO. Ranking higher on SERPs means increased visibility and more potential customers for your affiliate marketing campaigns.

9. Implementing Pay-Per-Click (PPC) Advertising:

Pay-per-click advertising is a popular strategy used by affiliate marketers to drive targeted traffic to their websites or landing pages. Platforms like Google Ads and Bing Ads allow you to bid on keywords and display ads to relevant audiences. While PPC can be expensive, it can yield quick results and complement your organic traffic efforts.

10. Tracking and Analyzing Performance:

Monitoring and analyzing your affiliate marketing performance is crucial for continuous improvement. Utilize tracking tools, such as Google Analytics and affiliate program analytics, to assess the effectiveness of your campaigns. Analyze your metrics, such as click-through rates, conversion rates, and revenue to identify areas for improvement and optimize your strategies accordingly.

Chapter 2 explored various affiliate marketing strategies that can help you build a successful and profitable affiliate marketing business. By selecting the right affiliate program, creating quality content, building an engaged audience, and leveraging different promotional channels, your chances of success will significantly increase. Remember, it is essential to continually adapt, analyze, and refine your strategies in this ever-evolving industry. In the upcoming chapters, we will further explore advanced approaches and techniques to take your affiliate marketing endeavors to the next level.

Decoding Affiliate Marketing Channels

In the ever-evolving world of digital marketing, affiliate marketing has emerged as a powerful strategy for brands and businesses to drive sales and expand their reach. With its ability to harness the influential power of individuals and organizations known as affiliates, this marketing channel has become an integral part of the marketing mix. In this chapter, we will delve into the intricacies of affiliate marketing channels, exploring their various forms, benefits, and implementation strategies. Join us as we uncover the secrets to effectively decode affiliate marketing channels.

What exactly is Affiliate Marketing?

Affiliate marketing is a performance-based marketing strategy where a business rewards its affiliates for each customer or visitor brought in through their promotional efforts. Affiliates, often popular bloggers, social media influencers, or websites, are equipped with unique affiliate links or promo codes to share with their audience. When a purchase is made using these links/codes, the affiliate earns a commission on the sale.

Affiliate marketing channels can take various forms depending on the platform used to promote products or services. Let's dive into the most common types of affiliate marketing channels.

1. Blogging and Content Marketing:

Blogs have long been a trusted source of information and recommendations for readers. As an affiliate marketing channel, blogs provide a compelling platform for affiliates to share product reviews, personal experiences, and curated lists of recommended items. By strategically placing affiliate links throughout their content, bloggers can earn a commission for purchases made from their referrals.

2. Social Media Influencers:

Social media platforms have witnessed exponential growth and have become a hub for influencers who wield considerable influence over their followers. Affiliates in this channel leverage their large and engaged social media following to promote products through sponsored posts, stories, or videos. When followers click on their unique affiliate links and make a purchase, the influencer earns a commission.

3. Coupon and Deal Websites:

In a world that thrives on discounts and deals, coupon and deal websites have found their niche in the affiliate marketing landscape. These websites gather and share the latest sales, promotions, and discount codes across various brands and industries. By using unique affiliate links or sharing exclusive promo codes, affiliates earn commissions when a sale is made through their referrals.

4. Comparison and Review Websites:

Consumers often turn to comparison and review websites to make informed purchasing decisions. Affiliates in this channel create unbiased and insightful reviews, comparing products or services within a specific niche. By including affiliate links to purchase the items being reviewed, these affiliates earn a commission when readers make a purchase through their recommendations.

5. Email Marketing:

Although considered a more traditional form of marketing, email marketing has found its place in the affiliate marketing realm. Affiliates build dedicated email lists and periodically send relevant offers, promotions, or product recommendations to their subscribers. When subscribers click on the affiliate links in these emails and proceed to make a purchase, the affiliate earns a commission.

6. Influencer Networks:

Influencer networks act as mediators between advertisers and influencers. These networks connect businesses with influencers whose audience aligns with the advertiser's target demographic. Influencer networks handle affiliate tracking, payments, and provide a streamlined experience for both affiliates and advertisers.

Benefits of Affiliate Marketing Channels:

Now that we understand the various types of affiliate marketing channels, let's explore some of the key benefits they bring to the table:

1. Cost-effective Advertising:

Affiliate marketing channels focus on performance-based marketing, meaning businesses only pay when a sale or desired action occurs. This makes it a cost-effective advertising solution as advertisers are assured a return on investment for marketing spends.

2. Wider Reach:

By leveraging the networks of affiliates, businesses can tap into a broader audience base that may have not been accessible through traditional marketing methods. Affiliates bring their own loyal followers who trust their recommendations, thus expanding the reach of a brand exponentially.

3. Enhanced Credibility and Trust:

Affiliates are often viewed as trustworthy sources of information, thanks to the relationships they have built with their audience. When they recommend a product or service, it is seen as a personal endorsement, fostering trust between the buyer and the brand.

4. Performance Tracking and Analytics:

Affiliate marketing channels provide businesses with detailed analytics and tracking capabilities. This allows advertisers to monitor and measure the performance of their campaigns in real-time, enabling them to optimize their strategies for better results.

Implementation Strategies:

Now that we understand the fundamentals and benefits of affiliate marketing channels, let's explore some key strategies for successful implementation:

1. Build Strong Relationships with Affiliates:

To ensure the success of your affiliate marketing campaigns, it is essential to build strong relationships with affiliates. Provide them with the necessary resources, such as high-quality promotional materials, exclusive discounts, and personalized support, to motivate them to promote your brand passionately.

2. Define Clear Objectives:

Before launching your affiliate marketing campaigns, it's crucial to define clear objectives. Determine what you want to achieve through affiliate marketing and clearly communicate these goals to your affiliates. It could be increased sales, brand visibility, new customer acquisition, or even lead generation.

3. Regularly Monitor and Optimize:

Keep a close eye on your campaign analytics, track conversions, and monitor the performance of your affiliates. Identify what's working and what's not, and make necessary adjustments to optimize your campaigns for better results. Regularly communicate with your affiliates to provide feedback and insights that can help them improve their promotional efforts.

4. Provide Compelling Incentives:

While affiliates earn commissions for successful referrals, providing additional incentives can go a long way in motivating them to prioritize your brand. Consider offering tiered commission structures, exclusive bonuses, or rewards for reaching specific sales targets to captivate and retain top-performing affiliates.

In this chapter, we explored the fascinating world of affiliate marketing channels. From blogging and social media influencers to coupon websites and email marketing, each channel offers unique advantages for businesses to connect with their target audience. By understanding the benefits and implementing effective strategies, brands can leverage the power of affiliates to drive sales, enhance brand credibility, and expand their reach in a highly competitive digital landscape.

Unleashing the Power of Content Marketing

In today's digital age, where information is readily available at our fingertips, consumers are becoming increasingly adept at filtering out traditional advertising methods. As a result, businesses have turned to content marketing as a powerful strategy to engage and connect with their target audience on a deeper level. This chapter explores the transformative potential of content marketing, shedding light on its key elements, benefits, and how to effectively implement this strategy to maximize its impact.

Understanding Content Marketing:

Content marketing is the art of creating and distributing valuable, relevant, and consistent content to attract and retain a clearly defined audience. It goes beyond promotional messages and focuses on delivering information that educates, entertains, or inspires your target audience.

Content comes in various forms, such as blog posts, videos, podcasts, infographics, e-books, and social media posts. The diverse range of formats allows businesses to cater to different audience preferences and provide a multi-dimensional experience to their customers.

The Role of Valuable Content:

One of the fundamental principles of content marketing is the creation of valuable content. Valuable content resonates with your audience, addressing their pain points, desires, and interests. By providing valuable insights and solutions, businesses position themselves as authorities in their industries, fostering trust and loyalty among their target audience.

Creating a Content Strategy:

To leverage the power of content marketing, it is crucial to have a well-defined content strategy. This involves understanding your target audience, identifying their needs and preferences, and creating content that aligns with their interests. In addition, determining the most suitable channels to distribute your content, be it through your website, social media platforms, or email newsletters, is a key component of an effective content strategy.

Developing Engaging Content:

Engaging content is essential for capturing and retaining your audience's attention. Storytelling, for instance, has proven to be a powerful tool in content marketing. By weaving narratives that connect with emotions, businesses can build deep and lasting relationships with their customers. Furthermore, incorporating elements such as humor, creativity, and interactivity into content can enhance engagement and make your brand more memorable.

Measuring Success with Analytics:

Analyzing the success of your content marketing efforts is vital in refining and optimizing your strategies. By utilizing tracking tools and analytics, businesses can measure the impact of their content, including metrics such as website traffic, social media engagement, conversions, and customer feedback. This data-driven approach helps identify areas for improvement and enables businesses to make informed decisions to enhance their content marketing efforts continuously.

Building Trust and Authority:

Content marketing plays a vital role in establishing your brand's trust and authority within your industry. By consistently providing valuable content, businesses can position themselves as thought leaders and go-to resources for their target audience. This authority not only increases customer loyalty but also attracts new prospects who trust your expertise.

Enhancing SEO and Organic Reach:

Search engine optimization (SEO) is a crucial aspect of content marketing. By producing high-quality content that incorporates relevant keywords and optimized meta tags, businesses can improve their visibility in search engine results pages. This increases organic traffic, enhances brand exposure, and ultimately contributes to the growth of the business.

Leveraging Social Media:

Social media platforms have become indispensable tools for content marketing. Creating compelling and shareable content on platforms such as Facebook, Instagram, Twitter, and LinkedIn expands your reach exponentially. Additionally, social media provides an avenue for businesses to engage directly with their audience, fostering authentic connections and generating valuable feedback.

Content Marketing in a Mobile World:

With the rise of smartphones and mobile browsing, content marketing has seen a shift towards mobile optimization. It is crucial for businesses to ensure their content is mobile-friendly, as users increasingly access information and consume content on their mobile devices. Responsive web design, fast-loading pages, and mobile-specific content are essential components of a successful content marketing strategy in today's mobile-driven world. Unleashing the power of content marketing requires not only delivering valuable content but also effectively engaging and connecting with your audience. By understanding your target audience, developing a comprehensive content strategy, and utilizing the vast array of platforms and formats, businesses can leverage content marketing to build brand loyalty, establish authority, and cultivate lasting customer relationships. With the right approach, content marketing has the potential to transform your business and capture the hearts and minds of your audience, giving you a competitive edge in the digital landscape.

The Role of Social Media in Affiliate Success

In today's digital age, social media has revolutionized the way people communicate, share information, and connect with others. Platforms such as Facebook, Instagram, Twitter, and LinkedIn have not only transformed the way we interact socially but have also influenced various aspects of our professional lives. One such area that has been significantly impacted is the realm of affiliate marketing, where social media has emerged as a powerful tool for driving success and generating revenue. In this chapter, we will explore the role of social media in affiliate success, delving into the strategies, benefits, challenges, and best practices to maximize its potential.

Understanding Social Media in Affiliate Marketing

Before diving into the details, it is essential to grasp the fundamentals of affiliate marketing and social media. Affiliate marketing refers to a performance-based marketing approach where businesses reward individuals (affiliates) for bringing them customers or generating sales through their marketing efforts. Social media, on the other hand, encompasses various online platforms and technologies that enable users to create and share content, connect with others, and engage in virtual communities. When combined, affiliate marketing through social media allows individuals to leverage their online presence, networks, and content creation skills to earn commissions and drive sales for businesses.

1. Leveraging Social Media Platforms

With numerous social media platforms available, it is crucial for affiliates to understand the strengths and characteristics of each platform to effectively promote and endorse products or services. Each platform has its own target audience, engagement styles, and content formats. For instance, Facebook offers a diverse user base, making it suitable for a wide range of products, while Instagram, being highly visual, is perfect for fashion, beauty, and lifestyle products. Twitter, with its concise and real-time nature, is great for promoting time-sensitive offers or news, whereas LinkedIn is primarily used for professional networking and B2B marketing.

2. Building an Engaged and Relevant Audience

The key to affiliate success on social media lies in building an engaged and relevant audience to whom you can promote products. It is essential to focus on quality over quantity when it comes to followers or connections. Instead of aiming for a massive but disinterested audience, affiliates should focus on cultivating a community that genuinely values their content and trusts their recommendations. This can be achieved by creating high-quality, valuable posts that authentically resonate with the target audience, making use of engaging visuals, carefully crafted captions, and interactive elements like polls or quizzes.

3. Creating Compelling Content

Content creation is at the heart of successful affiliate marketing on social media. Affiliates need to produce compelling, informative, and visually appealing content that grabs the attention of their audience and convinces them to take action. It is essential to strike a balance between promotional and educational content, ensuring that the audience feels you genuinely care about their needs rather than just selling them something. Videos, product reviews, tutorials, and comparison articles are all effective ways to provide valuable information while subtly endorsing products or services.

4. Building Trust and Authenticity

In a world where marketing messages constantly bombard consumers, trust and authenticity have become vital. Affiliates must establish themselves as credible sources, building trust and rapport with their audience. Honesty, transparency, and personal experiences go a long way in gaining followers' confidence. Disclosing affiliate relationships and openly addressing both pros and cons of products or services demonstrate integrity and ensure that the audience knows they are getting unbiased recommendations.

5. Leveraging Influencer Marketing

Influencer marketing has become an integral part of social media promotion and can significantly contribute to affiliate success. Businesses collaborate with influencers, who have a strong following and influence over their audience, to endorse products or services. Affiliates can leverage their position as influencers in their own right, and if they have a substantial following or niche authority, they can partner with brands for sponsored posts, product reviews, or giveaways. This not only helps generate revenue directly but also enhances credibility and expands reach, attracting more followers and potential customers.

In this chapter, we have explored the role of social media in affiliate marketing, shedding light on strategies, benefits, challenges, and best practices for success. However, it is worth noting that social media is a dynamic landscape that constantly evolves, requiring affiliates to adapt, experiment, and stay up to date with the latest trends and algorithms. Embracing social media as a powerful ally and leveraging its potentials can undoubtedly play a pivotal role in achieving affiliate success in today's digital age.

Exploring Paid Advertising for Affiliates

In the ever-evolving world of digital marketing, paid advertising has emerged as a powerful tool for affiliates to boost their visibility and drive targeted traffic to their websites. With a plethora of platforms and advertising options available, affiliates can strategically harness the potential of paid advertising to maximize their reach and generate substantial revenue. This chapter aims to delve into the intricacies of paid advertising for affiliates, exploring various platforms, strategies, and best practices to help affiliates navigate this dynamic landscape successfully.

Understanding Paid Advertising

Paid advertising refers to the practice of purchasing ad space on relevant websites, social media platforms, search engine result pages (SERPs), and other digital media to promote products or services. It offers affiliates a chance to reach a wider audience beyond organic search traffic.

Choosing the Right Advertising Platforms

To begin exploring paid advertising, affiliates must first identify the most suitable platforms that align with their target audience and niche. Below are some popular options worth considering:

1. Search Engine Advertising: Platforms like Google Ads and Microsoft Advertising (formerly Bing Ads) allow affiliates to create text-based ads that appear alongside search results when users search for relevant keywords. These ads can provide valuable visibility, especially for affiliates targeting high-intent audiences.

2. Social Media Advertising: Social media platforms like Facebook, Instagram, Twitter, and LinkedIn offer highly targeted advertising options. Affiliates can create visually appealing ads tailored to specific demographics, interests, and behaviors of their desired audience.

3. Display Advertising: Display ads are visually engaging banners, images, or videos that appear on various websites within a network. Platforms like Google Display Network (GDN) and programmatic ad exchanges provide extensive reach and targeting capabilities for affiliates.

4. Video Advertising: Video ads have gained significant popularity due to the rising prominence of platforms like YouTube. Affiliates can leverage video ads to engage users and showcase their products or services effectively.

5. Native Advertising: Native ads blend seamlessly into the content of a publisher's website, making them appear more organic and less intrusive. Affiliate networks like Outbrain and Taboola offer native advertising options, enabling affiliates to promote their offers subtly.

Developing a Paid Advertising Strategy

Once affiliates have chosen their desired advertising platforms, it is crucial to formulate a well-defined strategy to ensure optimum results. Here are some key steps to consider:

1. Define Objectives: Affiliates must establish clear objectives for their paid advertising campaign. Whether it is generating leads, increasing sales, driving app downloads, or building brand awareness, having well-defined goals will provide direction and allow for effective measurement of success.

2. Know Your Audience: Understanding the target audience is pivotal for creating compelling ads and ensuring maximum ROI. Affiliates should conduct thorough research to identify their audience's demographics, preferences, pain points, and online behavior. This information will help in tailoring ad messaging and choosing relevant targeting options.

3. Keyword Research: For search engine ads, extensive keyword research is crucial. Using tools like Google Keyword Planner or SEMrush, affiliates can identify relevant keywords with high search volume and low competition. Incorporating these keywords into ad copy and landing pages can improve ad relevance and quality score, leading to better ad placement and lower costs.

4. Crafting Engaging Ad Content: Ad content should be concise,

persuasive, and attention-grabbing, ensuring it aligns with the tone and brand image of the affiliate. Visual elements, such as high-quality images or videos, can significantly enhance ad performance, capturing users' interest and encouraging them to take action.

5. Implementing Effective Landing Pages: Creating dedicated, well-designed landing pages that align with the ad content is essential for driving conversions. Landing pages should provide clear calls-to-action (CTAs), highlight the value proposition, and minimize distractions to ensure a seamless user experience.

6. Setting Budgets and Bids: To optimize advertising spend, it is crucial to set realistic budgets and bids. Affiliates must monitor and adjust bid amounts based on the performance of various keywords, ad placements, and targeting options. Experimenting with different bidding strategies, such as Cost Per Click (CPC) or Cost Per Thousand Impressions (CPM), can help refine and optimize campaigns.

7. Monitoring and Analyzing Performance: Regularly monitoring key performance indicators (KPIs) is vital to gauge the effectiveness of paid advertising efforts. Tracking metrics like click-through rates (CTR), conversion rates, return on ad spend (ROAS), and cost per acquisition (CPA) allows affiliates to identify underperforming ads or campaigns early on and make data-driven optimizations.

Optimizing Paid Advertising Campaigns

Affiliates must continuously optimize their paid advertising campaigns to maximize their return on investment. Here are some optimization strategies to consider:

1. Ad Fatigue Management: Over time, ad fatigue can occur when the same creative or message is repeatedly shown to the target audience. To combat this, affiliates should regularly refresh their ad content or rotate multiple variations to maintain engagement and minimize ad blindness.

2. A/B Testing: Conducting A/B tests enables affiliates to compare different ad variations, landing pages, or targeting options to identify the most effective combinations. By testing variables like headlines, call-to-action buttons, colors, or ad placements, affiliates can make informed decisions based on quantifiable data.

3. Remarketing and Retargeting: Leveraging remarketing and retargeting tactics allows affiliates to re-engage users who have previously interacted with their ads or visited their website. By segmenting these users and delivering personalized ads, affiliates can increase brand recall and conversion rates.

4. Ad Placement Optimization: Analyzing the performance of ads across different placements, websites, or devices is crucial. Affiliates should identify high-performing placements and allocate more

budget accordingly while excluding low-performing ones. Additionally, optimizing ads for different devices, such as smartphones or tablets, can cater to specific user behaviors and preferences.

5. Earning Trust and Relevance: Ad performance can be significantly enhanced by establishing trust and relevance. By adhering to ethical practices and complying with advertising guidelines, affiliates can build a positive reputation and increase user trust. Furthermore, ensuring that ads are relevant, targeted, and aligned with the target audience's needs will lead to higher engagement and conversion rates.

Paid advertising has become an indispensable tool in the affiliate marketing arsenal, offering affiliates a way to amplify their reach, drive targeted traffic, and increase their revenue potential. By strategically selecting suitable platforms, formulating well-defined strategies, and continuously optimizing campaigns, affiliates can unlock the full potential of paid advertising. As the digital landscape continues to evolve, affiliates must stay agile, adapt to emerging trends, and leverage data-driven insights to achieve long-term success in this competitive space.

Chapter 3: Building Trust and Credibility as an Affiliate Marketer

In the world of affiliate marketing, trust and credibility are crucial elements that can make or break your success as an affiliate marketer. Building a reputable online presence and establishing trust with your audience is imperative if you want to thrive in this highly competitive industry. This chapter will provide you with valuable insights and strategies to build trust and establish credibility as an affiliate marketer.

Understanding the Importance of Trust and Credibility

Trust is the bedrock of any successful relationship, and the same holds true for the relationship between an affiliate marketer and their audience. When people trust you, they are more likely to take your recommendations seriously, purchase products through your affiliate links, and even become loyal followers.

Credibility is closely intertwined with trust, as it refers to the perception of your expertise, authenticity, and reliability. A credible affiliate marketer is seen as a knowledgeable resource that provides valuable insights and recommendations. Without trust and credibility, your efforts as an affiliate marketer will be in vain, and you will struggle to gain traction in a highly competitive marketplace.

Now, let's explore some proven strategies to help you build trust and credibility as an affiliate marketer.

1. Be Transparent and Authentic

One of the most critical elements of building trust and credibility is being transparent and authentic with your audience. Be open about the fact that you are an affiliate marketer, and clearly disclose your affiliations when promoting products or services. This transparency will foster trust by establishing an honest and open relationship with your audience.

Additionally, authenticity is key to building credibility. Share your personal experiences and opinions genuinely, so your audience can relate to you on a more human level. People appreciate honest recommendations, and real stories will resonate more strongly with them.

2. Provide Valuable and Relevant Content

To establish trust and credibility, focus on delivering high-quality, valuable content that is relevant to your target audience. This content can take various forms, such as blog posts, videos, podcasts, or social media updates. Your content should be informative, engaging, and solve a problem or address a need your audience has.

Make sure to conduct thorough research and provide accurate information in your content. Being a reliable source of information will enhance your credibility and position you as an authority in your niche.

3. Build a Personal Brand

Building a strong personal brand is instrumental in gaining trust and credibility as an affiliate marketer. A personal brand represents your unique personality, expertise, and values. It distinguishes you from other affiliate marketers and helps you connect with your audience on a deeper level.

Invest time in developing your personal brand by defining your mission, identifying your target audience, and consistently aligning your messaging and content with your brand values. This will establish your credibility and make you more relatable to your audience, leading to higher trust levels.

4. Establish Relationships and Engage with Your Audience

Building meaningful relationships and engaging with your audience is a powerful way to cultivate trust and credibility. Encourage your audience to interact with you through comments, emails, or social media channels, and make it a priority to respond promptly and sincerely. This shows your audience that you value their input and are genuinely interested in their thoughts and concerns.

Developing relationships with other influencers and professionals in your niche is also crucial for building trust and credibility. Collaborating with these individuals, sharing their content, or participating in joint ventures can provide a boost to your reputation and lend you credibility by association.

5. Review and Test Products

Another effective way to build trust and credibility is by providing honest and unbiased product reviews. Take the time to thoroughly test products before recommending them to your audience. Sharing your genuine experiences and highlighting both positives and negatives will demonstrate your honesty and integrity.

As you review and test products, consider the needs and preferences of your audience. Your recommendations should align with their interests, solving their problems and enhancing their lives. Tailoring your recommendations with their best interests in mind will strengthen the bond of trust between you and your audience.

6. Offer Bonuses and Incentives

Offering bonuses and incentives can significantly aid in building trust and credibility. This includes providing additional value to your audience when they make a purchase through your affiliate links. This value could be in the form of exclusive content, e-books, video tutorials, or discounts.

When you offer something extra, it showcases your commitment to your audience's satisfaction and enhances their overall experience. They will recognize your efforts and perceive you as a trusted affiliate marketer invested in their success.

7. Continuously Educate Yourself

Investing in your education and staying updated in your industry is vital for building trust and credibility. Demonstrating that you are committed to continuously learning and improving your knowledge will solidify your position as an expert in your niche.

Make it a habit to read industry blogs, attend webinars, listen to podcasts, and participate in relevant courses or conferences. Share the valuable insights you gain with your audience, showing that you are always striving to provide them with the most accurate and up-to-date information.

In the world of affiliate marketing, trust and credibility are paramount. Building a reputable online presence requires transparency, authenticity, valuable content, a strong personal brand, engagement with your audience, unbiased product reviews, the offer of bonuses and incentives, and continuous education. By implementing these strategies, you can establish trust and credibility, paving the way for long-term success as an affiliate marketer.

The Trust Factor in Affiliate Marketing

In today's digital era, affiliate marketing has emerged as a promising avenue for individuals and businesses looking to generate passive income. As the online landscape continues to evolve, building trust with your audience becomes paramount. Establishing credibility and maintaining a strong reputation is what sets successful affiliates apart from the crowd. In this chapter, we delve into the trust factor in affiliate marketing, exploring its significance, strategies to foster trust, and the long-term benefits it brings.

1. The Importance of Trust in Affiliate Marketing:

1.1 Authenticity and Credibility:
Trust is the foundation of any successful relationship, and affiliate marketing is no exception. As an affiliate marketer, your audience relies on your recommendations and expertise to make informed purchasing decisions. By establishing yourself as an authentic and credible source, you instill confidence in potential customers, making them more likely to convert. Genuine enthusiasm, transparency, and a reputation for endorsing quality products can help solidify this trust.

1.2 Building Long-Term Relationships:
Affiliate marketing is not a one-time transaction. Successful affiliates aim to build long-term relationships with their audience and the

brands they represent. Trust is crucial for nurturing such relationships. When your audience trusts your recommendations, they are more likely to return for future purchases, providing a steady stream of passive income. Additionally, cultivating trust with brands can lead to exclusive partnership opportunities and higher commission rates.

2. Strategies to Foster Trust in Affiliate Marketing:

2.1 Producing High-Quality Content:
Creating valuable and relevant content is crucial for building trust. By consistently delivering informative and engaging material, you position yourself as an expert in your niche. Offer in-depth product reviews, tutorials, and informative articles that genuinely help your audience. This demonstrates your commitment to providing real value and builds trust over time. Remember, high-quality content reinforces your credibility and showcases your dedication to helping your audience make informed choices.

2.2 Genuine Recommendations:
Transparency is key when making product recommendations. Carefully vet any product or service you endorse before promoting it to your audience. Only recommend products that you trust and genuinely believe will benefit your audience. Clearly disclose any affiliate relationships and be upfront about receiving a commission. Authenticity in your recommendations will enhance your audience's trust in your judgment, fostering long-term loyalty.

2.3 Social Proof and Testimonials:

Leveraging social proof and testimonials can significantly enhance the trust factor in affiliate marketing. Encourage satisfied customers to provide testimonials praising the products or services you endorse. Display these testimonials prominently on your website or social media platforms. Additionally, incorporating user-generated content, such as customer reviews or success stories, can further validate your recommendations. Social proof is a powerful tool that convinces potential customers of the product's value, bolstering trust.

2.4 Transparency with Affiliate Links:

Making your affiliate links explicit and transparent is essential for building trust. Clearly disclose affiliate links within your content, indicating that you may receive a commission from qualifying purchases. Failing to disclose affiliate relationships may erode your audience's trust and damage your reputation. Ensure that your audience understands the relationship between your content and any affiliate links, promoting transparency and fostering trust.

2.5 Consistent Engagement and Communication:

Regularly engaging with your audience is crucial for building trust. Respond to their comments, questions, and concerns promptly and authentically. People appreciate being heard and valued, and open communication fosters trust and credibility. Maintain an active presence on social media platforms and email newsletters to provide ongoing support, engage in meaningful conversations, and address any customer issues promptly. A consistent and reliable presence will strengthen your bond with your audience.

3. The Long-Term Benefits:

3.1 Repeat Business and Referrals:
Building trust as an affiliate marketer yields long-term benefits, such as repeat business and referrals. When customers trust your recommendations, they are more likely to return to your platform for future purchases. Satisfied customers may also refer your content and products to their friends and family, effectively expanding your audience. An established reputation for trustworthiness can drive sustained income by cultivating customer loyalty and encouraging organic growth.

3.2 Increased Affiliate Opportunities:
Trust facilitates collaborations with reputable brands and opens doors to new affiliate opportunities. Brands are more inclined to partner with affiliates who have a proven record of trustworthiness, allowing you to expand your repertoire of products and services. As your influence grows, you may negotiate higher commission rates, exclusive discounts, or even become an affiliate ambassador for specific companies. Trust empowers you to establish mutually beneficial partnerships and unlock lucrative opportunities.

3.3 Authority and Influence:
By consistently building trust, you establish yourself as an authority

in your niche. As your reputation grows, your audience perceives you as a reliable and knowledgeable resource. This authority and influence can extend beyond affiliate marketing, potentially leading to speaking engagements, guest posts, or collaboration opportunities with industry leaders. Building trust unlocks pathways to diversified income streams and positions you as a sought-after expert in your field.

Building trust is an ongoing process in affiliate marketing that requires consistent effort, transparency, and authenticity. By prioritizing the trust factor, you foster long-term relationships with your audience, leading to repeat business, referrals, and increased affiliate opportunities. Embrace the strategies outlined in this chapter to establish yourself as a trusted affiliate marketer and unlock the full potential of your online influence. Remember, trust is the bedrock upon which profitable and sustainable affiliate marketing endeavors are built.

Crafting High-Quality and Trustworthy Content

In the age of information overload, creating high-quality and trustworthy content has become more critical than ever. With millions of articles, blog posts, videos, and social media updates published every day, it is essential to stand out and earn the trust of your audience. In this chapter, we will explore the key principles and strategies for crafting content that is not only valuable but also resonates with your readers and establishes your credibility as an author.

Understanding Your Audience:

The foundation of creating compelling content lies in understanding your audience. Before you start writing, take the time to research and analyze your target demographic. Consider their needs, interests, and pain points. This knowledge will serve as your guiding compass, helping you tailor your content to their preferences, making it relevant and engaging.

Research and Credibility:

High-quality content is backed by thorough research and reliable sources. Before sharing information, verify the credibility and accuracy of your sources. Reputable studies, peer-reviewed articles, and expert opinions add credibility to your content and position you as a trusted authority. Always fact-check your claims and ensure that your information is up to date.

Structuring Your Content:

Crafting content that is easy to consume is just as important as producing high-quality information. Consider your target audience's reading habits and preferences when structuring your content. Break your text into scannable sections with subheadings, use bullet points for key information, and utilize formatting techniques such as bold or italicized fonts to emphasize important ideas. By optimizing your content's readability, you can enhance your audience's comprehension and overall satisfaction.

Attention-Grabbing Headlines:

An attention-grabbing headline is often the difference between someone clicking to read your content or scrolling past it. Craft your headlines carefully to pique curiosity and provide a clear benefit or value proposition. Use action words, numbers, and emotionally compelling language to entice your readers to delve deeper into your content. However, it is important to strike a balance between creating catchy headlines and delivering on the promised value within your content.

Engaging Once you have successfully captured your reader's attention with an enticing headline, it's crucial to keep them hooked with an engaging introduction. Begin by addressing the reader's pain points or desires and introducing the topic in a way that resonates on a personal level. A strong opening will create an emotional connection, motivating your audience to continue reading and explore the depths of your content.

Providing Value:

To create high-quality content, the foremost focus should be on providing value to your readers. Whether it's actionable tips, in-depth analysis, or unique insights, every piece of content must offer something that the reader can take away and apply. Consider their informational needs and problems, and deliver content that serves as a solution, giving them a reason to trust your expertise and come back for more.

Storytelling and Emotion:

Humans are wired to respond to stories. Incorporate storytelling techniques into your content to evoke emotions and create a deeper connection with your audience. Use anecdotes, case studies, or personal experiences to illustrate your points, making them relatable and engaging. Emotional resonance not only keeps readers invested but also helps them remember and share your content with others, amplifying its reach and impact.

Visual Enhancement:

Visual elements such as images, infographics, and videos can significantly enhance the impact and appeal of your content. Incorporate relevant visuals that complement and reinforce your message. Well-placed images help break up text and provide visual relief, while infographics and videos can effectively communicate complex concepts or data in a concise and engaging manner. However, ensure that all visuals used are high-quality, relevant, and properly sourced to maintain your credibility.

Authenticity and Transparency:

Building trust with your audience requires authenticity and transparency. Be genuine and transparent in your communication, admitting your limitations and biases when necessary. Acknowledge and respond to readers' comments and feedback, fostering a sense of connection and dialogue. Honesty and openness will establish you as a trustworthy and reliable source of information, strengthening the bond with your audience.

Originality and Uniqueness:

The digital realm is saturated with content, making it crucial to bring your authentic voice and unique perspective. Aim to offer insights, knowledge, or opinions that are distinct and differentiate you from the competition. Conduct original research, share personal experiences, or take unconventional angles to provide fresh content that adds value and sparks intrigue.

Optimizing for Search Engines:

Creating high-quality content alone is not enough; you must ensure that it reaches your intended audience. Incorporate basic search engine optimization (SEO) techniques to make your content discoverable. Identify relevant keywords and strategically incorporate them throughout your content, including in headings, meta tags, and image alt text. Crafting an enticing meta description can significantly impact your click-through rate from search engine results pages, driving organic traffic to your content.

Crafting high-quality and trustworthy content is no simple task, but it is a journey worth embarking on. By understanding your audience, conducting thorough research, and structuring your content effectively, you can captivate readers and earn their trust. Emphasize the importance of providing value, engaging storytelling, and authenticity. Remember, the key to creating content that stands the test of time lies in establishing a strong connection with your readers and consistently delivering content that surpasses their expectations.

Nurturing Authentic Relationships with Your Audience

In today's digital era, building and maintaining authentic relationships with your audience is more critical than ever. With countless platforms and channels available, it may seem challenging to stand out and connect with your target audience genuinely. However, by adopting certain strategies and approaches, you can cultivate meaningful relationships with your audience that will not only bolster your brand but also create a loyal customer base. In this chapter, we will explore techniques and best practices for nurturing authentic relationships with your audience and discuss the importance of empathy, engagement, and transparency.

Section 1: Understanding Your Audience:

Before embarking on any journey to nurture genuine relationships, it is vital to have a deep understanding of your audience. Understanding their needs, wants, behaviors, and preferences will lay the foundation for effective communication. Conducting thorough market research, leveraging analytics, and engaging with your audience directly through surveys or focus groups can provide invaluable insights. By clearly defining your target audience, you can personalize your strategies accordingly and ensure your messaging resonates with them on a personal level.

Section 2: Empathy as a Foundation:

Empathy is the cornerstone of building authentic relationships with your audience. It involves understanding and sharing the feelings, perspectives, and experiences of others. By demonstrating empathy, you show your audience that you genuinely care about their challenges and aspirations. This can be achieved through active listening, responding to feedback, and addressing their concerns promptly. When communicating with your audience, strive to create an emotional connection that goes beyond a transactional relationship.

Section 3: Engaging Your Audience:

Creating engaging content is paramount in nurturing authentic relationships. It's not enough to simply broadcast messages; you must actively seek ways to interact with your audience. Encourage feedback, ask thought-provoking questions, and provide educational or entertaining content that sparks conversation. Hosting live Q&A sessions, webinars, or virtual events can also help foster a sense of community and make your audience feel valued. Actively responding to comments, messages, and mentions across various platforms will further strengthen the connection with your audience.

Section 4: Personalization and Tailored Experiences:

In the age of automation, personalization is highly valued by consumers. Tailoring experiences to meet individuals' specific needs and preferences demonstrates that you see them as unique individuals rather than just part of a mass audience. Utilize data and analytics to personalize your communication, offering tailored recommendations, content, or offers based on their previous interactions. Personalized experiences foster a sense of connection and loyalty, as your audience knows that you understand and value them on a personal level.

Section 5: Transparency and Authenticity:

Authenticity is a fundamental element of nurturing relationships. Being transparent and honest about your brand values, processes, and even challenges builds trust and credibility. Share stories of success and failure, demonstrate vulnerability, and admit mistakes when necessary. Showing transparency not only humanizes your brand but also makes your audience feel like they are part of an honest conversation. Consumers today seek authenticity and are more likely to engage and stay loyal to brands that demonstrate it consistently.

Section 6: Consistency and Reliability:

Consistency is key in nurturing authentic relationships. By maintaining a consistent tone, messaging, and branding across all channels, you create a sense of familiarity and reliability. This consistency should extend to response times, delivering on promises, and providing a seamless customer experience. When your audience knows that they can depend on you, they are more likely to engage and develop long-term relationships. Consistency reinforces trust and strengthens your brand's reputation.

Section 7: Collaboration and Co-creation:

Collaboration with your audience can be a powerful driver of authentic relationships. Involve your audience in decision-making processes, seek their input on new products or services, and actively listen to their ideas. Co-creation not only makes your audience feel valued and included but also fosters a sense of ownership. By involving your audience in the creative process, you strengthen their connection and loyalty towards your brand. Collaborative efforts can also lead to innovative solutions and a competitive advantage.

Section 8: Going Beyond Transactions:

To truly nurture authentic relationships, aim to go beyond transactional interactions. Understand your audience's journey and support them every step of the way. Offer exceptional customer service, provide value through educational resources, and celebrate their successes. By showing genuine interest in their progress and wellbeing, you create a lasting bond that extends beyond a single purchase. Building relationships based on mutual growth and support will lead to long-term loyalty and advocacy.

Nurturing authentic relationships with your audience is a continuous process that requires effort, empathy, and dedication. By understanding your audience, demonstrating empathy, engaging with them, personalizing experiences, being transparent, maintaining consistency, collaborating, and going beyond transactions, you can build relationships that withstand the test of time. As you embark on this journey, remember to always put your audience at the forefront and focus on creating meaningful connections.

Utilizing Transparency to Strengthen Credibility

In today's fast-paced and interconnected world, credibility is an essential aspect of any individual or organization's success. Establishing and nurturing trust with stakeholders, customers, and partners is crucial for long-term growth and sustainability. In recent years, there has been a growing realization that transparency plays a pivotal role in building and maintaining credibility. By providing openness and honesty, transparency fosters trust and confidence, enabling organizations and individuals to thrive in an increasingly competitive landscape. This chapter will explore the importance of transparency in strengthening credibility and discuss various strategies to effectively utilize transparency as a powerful tool.

Understanding Transparency

Transparency, at its core, entails being open, truthful, and forthcoming in one's actions, decisions, and communication. It involves providing information in a clear and accessible manner, essentially allowing others to gain insight into the motives, processes, and outcomes of an individual or organization's operations. Transparency can take many forms, including sharing financial information, disclosing business practices, making decisions publicly, and actively engaging with stakeholders. The underlying principle is that transparency encourages accountability, fosters trust, and enhances credibility.

Transparency as a Catalyst for Trust

Trust is the foundation upon which relationships, both personal and professional, are built. Without trust, it becomes challenging to establish credibility. Transparency acts as a catalyst for trust by providing stakeholders with the necessary visibility into an individual or organization's actions and decisions. When people have access to information, they feel empowered and can make informed decisions based on the facts presented. Transparency eliminates the uncertainty and ambiguity that often leads to suspicion and doubt. By openly sharing information, organizations and individuals demonstrate their integrity, and stakeholders are more likely to trust their motives and actions.

The Benefits of Transparency

1. Enhanced Reputation: Transparency is a key driver of an organization's reputation. When organizations are transparent about their practices, performance, and values, stakeholders view them as trustworthy and reliable. This positive perception strengthens the organization's reputation, attracting customers, investors, and employees.

2. Improved Decision-Making: Transparency fosters an environment of openness and collaboration. When information is readily

available, individuals can make better-informed decisions. This applies not only to employees within an organization but also to customers who can evaluate products and services based on transparent and reliable information.

3. Increased Stakeholder Engagement: Transparency encourages stakeholders to actively participate and engage with an organization. By sharing information and inviting feedback, organizations demonstrate their commitment to inclusivity and collaboration. This engagement can lead to valuable insights, innovative ideas, and stronger relationships.

4. Crisis Management: Transparency plays a vital role during times of crisis. In situations where mistakes or failures occur, organizations that are transparent about the issue, its causes, and the steps being taken to address it, are more likely to regain trust and recover their credibility. By acknowledging mistakes rather than concealing them, organizations demonstrate accountability and a commitment to learning and improvement.

Strategies for Utilizing Transparency

1. Open Communication Channels: Establishing open lines of communication is crucial for practicing transparency. Whether it is within an organization or with external stakeholders, providing opportunities for dialogue and feedback ensures that information flows freely. Regularly updating stakeholders on progress,

challenges, and decisions helps build trust and confidence.

2. Active Engagement: Actively engaging stakeholders in decision-making processes demonstrates a commitment to transparency. For example, involving employees in critical business decisions or seeking input from customers on product development not only shows the value placed on their opinions but also fosters a sense of ownership and investment in the outcomes.

3. Sharing Information: Transparency is closely tied to sharing information openly and honestly. Organizations can make use of various platforms, including websites, annual reports, social media, and public statements to provide easy access to relevant information. Making financial data, performance metrics, and business practices accessible to stakeholders reinforces credibility and helps them make well-informed judgments.

4. Acknowledging Mistakes and Learning: Organizations and individuals need to embrace a culture that acknowledges mistakes and learns from them. Transparently communicating errors or failures, along with the steps taken to rectify them, demonstrates accountability and a commitment to improvement. This culture promotes a learning mindset and signals to stakeholders that the focus is on continuous growth rather than avoiding responsibility.

5. Adopting Ethical Practices: Transparency goes hand in hand with ethical behavior. Organizations need to demonstrate integrity in

their actions, ensuring that ethical guidelines and standards are met. Embracing ethical business practices fosters trust, as stakeholders can be confident that an organization's actions align with their stated values.

Transparency is no longer a buzzword; it has become an essential aspect of building and maintaining credibility in today's society. By embracing transparency, organizations and individuals can establish trust, enhance reputation, and foster active engagement with stakeholders. The strategies discussed in this chapter provide a starting point for utilizing transparency effectively. When transparency becomes an integral part of an organization's culture, it becomes a powerful tool that helps strengthen credibility, leading to sustained success and growth.

Chapter 4: Navigating the Digital Marketplace for Affiliate Success

Welcome to Chapter 4 of our comprehensive guide on affiliate marketing! In this chapter, we will dive deep into the digital marketplace and explore the strategies necessary for an affiliate marketer to achieve success. The digital marketplace has revolutionized the way we conduct business, making it essential for affiliates to navigate this dynamic landscape effectively. By the end of this chapter, you will have a solid understanding of the key aspects of the digital marketplace and how to utilize its resources to maximize your affiliate marketing endeavors.

1. Embracing the Digital Marketplace:

The digital marketplace encompasses a vast array of platforms, such as websites, social media networks, search engines, and mobile applications. As an affiliate marketer, it is crucial to recognize the immense potential and reach that these platforms offer. To succeed in the digital marketplace, you must fully embrace its dynamics and keep pace with the ever-evolving trends and technologies shaping it.

2. Understanding Affiliate Networks:

Affiliate networks serve as the core infrastructure of the digital marketplace. These networks act as intermediaries, connecting affiliates with merchants and enabling the monetization of online traffic. When selecting an affiliate network, carefully consider factors such as reputation, commission rates, payout methods, and available marketing materials. It is important to align yourself with a reliable and trustworthy affiliate network to build a strong foundation for successful partnerships.

3. Choosing the Right Affiliate Program:

In the digital marketplace, countless affiliate programs exist, catering to a multitude of niches and industries. Selecting the right affiliate program is crucial as it determines the products or services you promote and the commissions you receive. Take adequate time to research and understand the potential of various affiliate programs in your chosen niche. Look for programs that align with your target audience's interests and offer high-quality products or services. Remember, choosing the right affiliate program is the first step towards long-term success.

4. Utilizing Effective Content Marketing:

Content marketing plays a pivotal role in the digital marketplace. By creating compelling, relevant, and valuable content, you can attract visitors to your website or social media channels. This, in turn, increases the likelihood of generating conversions and earning commissions. Great content can be in the form of blog posts, articles, product reviews, videos, or social media posts. Focus on producing content that engages your audience, provides useful information, and promotes the affiliate products or services effectively.

5. Harnessing the Power of Search Engine Optimization (SEO):

Search Engine Optimization (SEO) is fundamental for any online marketing initiative, including affiliate marketing. Properly optimizing your website and content can improve your search engine rankings and visibility, leading to increased organic traffic. By understanding keywords, meta tags, backlinks, and other SEO strategies, you can enhance your website's chances of appearing at the top of search engine results pages. Remember, the higher your website ranks, the more likely it is to attract visitors and generate conversions.

6. Leveraging Social Media Platforms:

With billions of users worldwide, social media platforms offer tremendous opportunities for affiliate marketers. Establishing a strong presence on popular social media channels such as Facebook, Instagram, Twitter, and LinkedIn can help you reach a vast audience, build a loyal following, and drive traffic to your affiliate offers. Craft engaging posts, share valuable content, and interact with your audience to build relationships and establish credibility. Social media's real-time nature allows for immediate interactions and response, making it a powerful tool for affiliate success.

7. Embracing Influencer Marketing:

Influencer marketing is an effective strategy in the digital marketplace that involves partnering with influential individuals in your niche. These influencers leverage their credibility, expertise, and large following to promote products or services. By aligning yourself with relevant influencers, you can tap into their loyal audiences and enhance your brand's visibility. Collaborating with influencers can significantly boost your affiliate marketing efforts and generate higher conversions.

8. Monitoring, Analyzing, and Tweaking Your Campaigns:
In the ever-changing landscape of the digital marketplace, constant monitoring, analyzing, and tweaking of your affiliate marketing campaigns are essential. Utilize analytics tools to track important metrics such as website traffic, click-through rates, conversion rates, and ROI. Identify what is working well and what needs improvement in your campaigns. By analyzing data and making necessary adjustments, you can optimize your efforts and ensure long-term success.

In this chapter, we have explored the digital marketplace and the strategies necessary for affiliate success in this dynamic landscape. Remember, embracing the digital marketplace, understanding affiliate networks, choosing the right affiliate program, utilizing effective content marketing, harnessing the power of SEO, leveraging social media, embracing influencer marketing, and monitoring and analyzing your campaigns are key ingredients for thriving in the digital marketplace. By implementing these strategies and staying updated on industry trends, you can pave your path to long-term affiliate marketing success.

Choosing the Right Affiliate Products or Services

In the ever-evolving world of affiliate marketing, choosing the right products or services to promote is vital for success. As an affiliate marketer, your ultimate goal is to generate income through commissions by promoting and selling other companies' products or services. However, with countless options available, selecting the right affiliate products requires a strategic approach that aligns with your target audience's needs and interests. This chapter will delve into the process of choosing the ideal affiliate products or services and provide valuable insights to enhance your affiliate marketing journey.

Understanding Your Target Audience:

When it comes to affiliate marketing, understanding your target audience is the key to success. Before choosing any affiliate products or services, it is crucial to thoroughly research and analyze your audience's preferences, demographics, psychographics, and behaviors. By gaining insights into your target audience, you can align your offerings with their needs, increasing the likelihood of conversions and generating revenue.

Market Research:

Effective market research plays a crucial role in identifying potential affiliate products or services that will resonate with your audience. Begin by identifying your niche market and its evolving trends. Utilize online tools, such as Google Trends, to gain insights into popular search terms and emerging trends related to your niche. This research will help you identify potential affiliate products or services that are in high demand.

Product Relevance:

While selecting affiliate products or services, relevance is paramount. Ensure that the products or services you choose align closely with your niche and target audience's interests. If your website or blog focuses on health and wellness, promoting products related to fitness equipment or nutritious recipes would be more relevant compared to unrelated items such as electronics.

Authenticity and Trustworthiness:

As an affiliate marketer, building trust with your audience is of utmost importance. Research, use, and review the products or services you plan to promote to ensure they meet your quality standards. By authenticating the offerings, you can genuinely recommend them to your audience, fostering trust and credibility. Promoting genuine and valuable products will reflect positively on your reputation, leading to a higher conversion rate.

Quality and Value:

The affiliate products or services you choose must offer excellent quality and value to your audience. Your reputation as an affiliate marketer depends on the perceived value of the products you promote. Prioritize products and services that have positive reviews, good customer service, and provide tangible benefits. Ensuring your promotions provide genuine value to your audience will maximize the chances of generating recurring sales and customer loyalty.

Commission Rates:

While commission rates should not be the sole determining factor, they play a significant role in choosing the right affiliate products or services. Compare commission rates across various affiliate programs to assess the potential return on investment for your promotional efforts. However, it's essential to strike a balance between competitive commissions and the relevance and value of the products or services to your audience.

Program Reliability and Stability:

Before partnering with any affiliate program, thoroughly research and evaluate their reliability and stability. The affiliate program should have a proven track record of timely and accurate commission payouts. Scrutinize their terms and conditions, ensure they have a solid support system, and assess the ease of integration into your website or promotional channels. Partnering with reputable and reliable affiliate programs will safeguard your business from potential fraudulent activities and affiliate program shut-downs.

Affiliate Program Restrictions:

Carefully review the terms and conditions of affiliate programs to understand any restrictions they may impose. Some affiliate programs may prohibit certain promotional methods or place geographical constraints on their offerings. Evaluate whether these restrictions align with your marketing strategies and target audience. Avoid partnering with programs that hinder your promotional efforts, as they can limit your ability to generate income.

Promotional Resources:

Consider the availability of promotional resources such as banners, videos, landing pages, and promotional tools provided by the affiliate program. These resources can significantly streamline your promotional efforts and enhance your overall marketing strategy. Having access to high-quality promotional materials ensures a consistent brand presence and saves time and effort in creating customized content.

Competitive Analysis:

Thoroughly researching your competitors and their chosen affiliate products or services can provide valuable insights into successful promotion strategies. Analyze the products they promote, their content marketing approaches, and engagement tactics. This analysis will help you identify potential gaps in the market that you can leverage and differentiate yourself from your competition.

Testing and Performance Tracking:

Even after carefully selecting affiliate products or services, continuous testing and performance tracking are crucial to optimize your marketing efforts. Monitor the performance of different offerings and promotional strategies to identify what works best for your audience. Consider using tracking tools, such as Google Analytics or specific affiliate program dashboards, to evaluate your conversion rates, click-through rates, and overall revenue generation.

In Selecting the right affiliate products or services is a strategic process that requires thorough research, knowledge of your target audience, and an understanding of market trends. By aligning the offerings with your audience's needs, upholding authenticity and trustworthiness, and prioritizing quality and value, you can increase your chances of success as an affiliate marketer. Remember to continuously evaluate and optimize your promotions based on performance tracking and stay updated on industry trends and market demands.

Researching Your Niche and Target Audience

Welcome to Chapter 4.2 of our comprehensive guide on building a successful business. In this chapter, we will explore the vital process of researching your niche and target audience. Understanding your niche and identifying your ideal customers is fundamental to creating a solid foundation for your business. So, let's dive into the world of market research and discover how it can empower your entrepreneurial journey!

Understanding Niche and Target Audience:

Before immersing ourselves in research, let's clarify what we mean by "niche" and "target audience." Your niche refers to a specific segment of the market that you will focus on and cater to with your products or services. Identifying your niche enables you to understand your customers' needs better and offer solutions that resonate with them.

Your target audience, on the other hand, consists of the individuals within your niche who are most likely to become your customers. These are the people who will find immense value in what you have to offer and who you need to communicate with effectively to drive sales and growth.

Now that we have established the importance of researching your niche and target audience, let's delve into the methods and strategies to carry out effective market research.

1. Analyzing Competitors:

One of the first steps in researching your niche is understanding your competition. Examine other businesses operating in your niche and analyze their products, marketing strategies, strengths, and weaknesses. This analysis provides valuable insights into the market landscape, allowing you to identify gaps that you can fill with a unique selling proposition (USP) of your own. By differentiating your business from competitors, you increase your chances of attracting your target audience.

2. Conduct Surveys and Interviews:

Surveys and interviews are powerful tools for gathering direct feedback from potential customers. Develop a questionnaire or interview script targeting individuals who fit your target audience profile. Seek their opinions, preferences, and pain points related to your niche. By doing so, you gain a deeper understanding of your customers, enabling you to tailor your products or services to precisely meet their needs.

3. Leverage Social Media:

In today's digital age, social media platforms offer unprecedented access to vast amounts of consumer data. Utilize social media platforms like Facebook, Twitter, and Instagram to gain insights into the target audience's behavior, interests, and purchasing habits.

Observe how they interact, respond, and engage with content related to your niche. This data will equip you to develop strategies that effectively target and resonate with your ideal customers.

4. Use Google Trends and Keyword Research:

Tap into the wealth of information offered by Google Trends and keyword research tools. These tools highlight popular search terms and trends related to your niche. By noting the frequency of searches and analyzing the keywords people use when looking for similar products or services, you gain critical insights into what your target audience is seeking. Incorporating these keywords into your website's content and marketing materials will improve your visibility and attract a larger audience.

5. Analyze Customer Behavior:

Understanding how your potential customers behave is vital in tailoring your marketing activities. Analyze data from your website analytics, heatmaps, and conversion funnels to gain insights into customer behavior patterns. Identify which pages they visit the most, how much time they spend on each page, and where they drop off from the conversion process. This data will help optimize your website, marketing campaigns, and sales funnel to increase conversions and maximize your marketing efforts' ROI.

6. Conduct Focus Groups:

Focus groups provide a unique opportunity to gather qualitative data from your target audience. Assemble a group of individuals who closely match your target audience and facilitate a structured discussion. Encourage participants to freely express their thoughts and opinions on topics related to your niche. By actively listening to their feedback, you can gain new perspectives, uncover pain points, and identify product improvements or marketing strategies that would resonate well.

7. Monitor Online Communities:

Online communities and forums specific to your niche can be treasure troves of information. Join relevant communities where your target audience is active and observe the discussions. Pay attention to common threads, recurring questions, and topics that generate the most engagement. This will help you gauge the interests, concerns, and desires of your potential customers, allowing you to align and optimize your offerings accordingly.

In this chapter, we have explored the vital process of researching your niche and target audience. Thorough market research is crucial for any business to not only survive but thrive. By analyzing competitors, conducting surveys and interviews, leveraging social media, using tools like Google Trends and analytics, facilitating focus groups, and monitoring online communities, you can develop a comprehensive understanding of your niche and target audience. Armed with this knowledge, you are better equipped to meet customer needs, stand out in the market, and drive business growth. Remember, effective research is an ongoing process, and regularly re-evaluating your niche and target audience is essential in staying ahead of the curve. So, embrace the power of research, and unlock the true potential of your business!

The Art of Effective Market Positioning

In today's fiercely competitive business landscape, effective market positioning has become a crucial aspect of any successful marketing strategy. The ability to position a product or service effectively can mean the difference between achieving market dominance or fading into obscurity. This chapter delves into the art of effective market positioning, exploring the key concepts, strategies, and techniques that can help businesses carve out a distinct and favorable position in the minds of consumers. By understanding the nuances of market positioning, organizations can develop targeted and impactful marketing campaigns to drive brand recognition, customer loyalty, and ultimately, business growth.

Defining Market Positioning

So, what exactly is market positioning? Market positioning refers to the process of creating an identity and image for a product or service within the minds of target consumers. It involves creating a unique position in the market that differentiates a brand from its competitors and resonates with the target audience. The goal of effective market positioning is to establish a distinctive value proposition and communicate it clearly to consumers, thereby influencing their perceptions and purchase decisions.

Understanding the Target Audience

Before embarking on a market positioning strategy, it is crucial to gain a deep understanding of the target audience. Conducting thorough market research can provide valuable insights into consumer needs, preferences, and behavior patterns. By segmenting the market based on demographics, psychographics, and other variables, organizations can tailor their positioning efforts to appeal directly to each subset of their target audience. This tailored approach ensures that the positioning efforts resonate with the specific needs and desires of the intended consumers.

Differentiation: The Key to Success

In a crowded marketplace, differentiation is the linchpin of effective market positioning. Organizations must identify unique attributes and features that set their product or service apart from competitors. This can include aspects such as superior quality, innovative technology, exceptional customer service, or a compelling brand story. Differentiation should be rooted in a deep understanding of customer pain points and desires, ensuring that the unique value proposition solves a genuine problem or fulfills a specific need. Furthermore, differentiation must be tangible, verifiable, and sustainable to instill confidence in consumers and establish a competitive advantage.

Crafting a Compelling Value Proposition

Once differentiation has been identified, it is essential to craft a compelling value proposition. The value proposition is a concise statement that encapsulates the unique benefits and value that the product or service offers to consumers. It should clearly communicate the specific problem it solves, the advantages it provides, and how it compares to alternative solutions. A well-crafted value proposition establishes a strong foundation for market positioning by succinctly conveying the brand's promise to consumers. It should resonate with the target audience and elicit an emotional connection, instilling confidence and a desire to engage with the brand.

Segmentation, Targeting, and Positioning

To effectively position a product or service in the market, businesses must adopt a strategic approach known as segmentation, targeting, and positioning (STP). Segmentation involves dividing the market into distinct groups based on common characteristics, needs, or preferences. This allows organizations to identify the most promising segments to focus their positioning efforts on.

Once segments are identified, the next step is targeting. Targeting involves selecting the most attractive segments to prioritize resources and marketing efforts. By focusing on specific segments, organizations can tailor their positioning efforts to resonate with the desires and demands of their chosen target audience, ultimately maximizing their marketing effectiveness.

Finally, positioning comes into play. Positioning entails creating a distinctive place or image for the brand within the minds of consumers. This involves considering factors such as price, product attributes, distribution channels, promotion strategies, and brand associations. Effective positioning requires aligning these elements to communicate the brand's unique value proposition clearly.

Building Emotional Connections

In today's hyperconnected world, building emotional connections between brands and consumers has become a critical factor in successful market positioning. Emotional connections go beyond functional benefits and tap into consumers' aspirations, values, and beliefs. By aligning a brand with consumers' emotional desires, organizations can create a deep-seated connection that drives loyalty, advocacy, and ultimately, increased market share.

To build emotional connections, brands must not only meet the rational needs of consumers but also appeal to their desires for social acceptance, self-esteem, or personal growth. This may involve leveraging storytelling techniques to create narratives that evoke emotions. It could also involve aligning the brand with social or environmental causes that resonate with the target audience. By tapping into these emotional aspects, brands can cultivate a sense of affinity and inspire consumer loyalty.

Testing and Monitoring

Once a market positioning strategy has been implemented, it is crucial to continually test and monitor its effectiveness. Regular market research, consumer feedback, and performance metrics provide insights into how the intended positioning message is resonating with the target audience. This information allows organizations to make necessary adjustments and refinements to ensure the market positioning remains effective over time.

Effective market positioning is a dynamic and multifaceted process that requires a deep understanding of the target audience, differentiation, compelling value propositions, and emotional appeal. By employing strategic segmentation, targeting, and positioning, organizations can establish a unique identity within the minds of consumers. Building emotional connections and consistently monitoring the strategy's performance ensures that market positioning remains relevant in an ever-evolving marketplace. With careful planning and execution, businesses can master the art of effective market positioning and propel their brands to new heights of success.

Leveraging Analytics to Optimize Your Strategy

In today's data-driven world, the ability to leverage analytics has become a critical factor for success in any business strategy. Analytics provides organizations with the power to extract valuable insights from vast amounts of data, enabling them to make informed decisions, improve efficiency, and gain a competitive edge. This chapter dives into the world of leveraging analytics to optimize your strategy, examining the key concepts, benefits, challenges, and best practices associated with this essential process.

Understanding Analytics:

Before we explore the ways in which analytics can optimize your strategy, it's crucial to establish a clear understanding of what analytics entails. Analytics refers to the systematic examination of data to uncover meaningful patterns, trends, and correlations. By harnessing various analytical techniques and tools, businesses can transform raw data into actionable insights that drive informed decision-making.

Types of Analytics:

Analytics can be broadly categorized into three types: descriptive, predictive, and prescriptive analytics. Descriptive analytics involves analyzing historical data to understand what happened in the past. It helps businesses gain insights into past performance, identify patterns, and track key performance indicators (KPIs).

Predictive analytics, on the other hand, leverages historical data and statistical algorithms to make predictions about future outcomes. By identifying trends and patterns, businesses can anticipate customer behavior, optimize inventory levels, and mitigate risks.

Prescriptive analytics takes things a step further by providing actionable recommendations based on predictive models and optimization algorithms. It enables organizations to make data-driven decisions that shape the future and maximize desired outcomes.

Benefits of Leveraging Analytics:

The strategic utilization of analytics offers several benefits for organizations seeking to optimize their strategies:

1. Informed Decision-Making: Analytics provides decision-makers with unbiased, data-driven insights, reducing the reliance on intuition and guesswork. This helps in making informed choices that align with organizational objectives.

2. Improved Efficiency: By identifying inefficiencies and bottlenecks, analytics enables businesses to streamline processes, eliminate

waste, and reduce costs. This improved efficiency ultimately
enhances overall productivity.

3. Competitive Advantage: Leveraging analytics offers organizations
a competitive edge by identifying untapped opportunities,
anticipating market trends, and understanding customer preferences
better. These insights allow businesses to stay ahead of the curve
and outperform their competitors.

4. Enhanced Personalization: Analytics enables businesses to
personalize their offerings according to customer preferences and
behavior. By understanding customer needs, organizations can tailor
their marketing campaigns, product recommendations, and
customer experiences, leading to increased customer satisfaction
and loyalty.

5. Risk Mitigation: Analytics plays a crucial role in identifying and
mitigating risks by uncovering patterns that indicate potential
threats. This proactive approach allows businesses to take
preventive measures, minimizing the negative impact of potential
risks.

Challenges in Leveraging Analytics:

While leveraging analytics can lead to numerous benefits,
organizations must navigate through several challenges to maximize
its potential:

1. Data Quality and Accessibility: Analytics heavily relies on accurate and accessible data. Poor data quality, incomplete datasets, and data silos can hinder the effectiveness of analytics initiatives. Organizations must invest in data management and governance processes to ensure data integrity and accessibility.

2. Resource Constraints: Effective utilization of analytics requires skilled personnel, appropriate infrastructure, and reliable software and tools. Acquiring and maintaining these resources can pose challenges for organizations, particularly smaller ones with limited budgets.

3. Scalability: As data volumes continue to grow, scalability becomes a significant challenge. Analyzing and processing large datasets within acceptable time frames can strain IT resources. Organizations must invest in scalable infrastructure and technologies to overcome this challenge.

4. Analytical Talent: The scarcity of skilled analysts poses a significant challenge for organizations. The demand for data scientists and analysts with expertise in statistical modeling, machine learning, and data visualization exceeds supply. Organizations need to invest in building and retaining analytical talent to support their strategic initiatives.

Best Practices for Leveraging Analytics:

To successfully leverage analytics and optimize your strategy, organizations should consider the following best practices:

1. Clearly Define Objectives: Before embarking on analytics initiatives, clearly define your strategic objectives. Identify the specific questions you want to answer and the goals you aim to achieve through analytics.

2. Establish Data Governance: Implement robust data governance processes to ensure data quality, consistency, and accessibility. Establish data ownership, standardize definitions, and encourage a data-driven culture within the organization.

3. Build Cross-Functional Teams: Form cross-functional teams comprising subject matter experts, data scientists, and business analysts. This collaboration helps bridge the gap between technical expertise and domain knowledge, enabling effective interpretation of analytics insights.

4. Leverage Advanced Analytics Techniques: Move beyond traditional analytics by adopting advanced techniques such as machine learning, natural language processing, and artificial intelligence. These techniques can unlock deeper insights and improve the accuracy of predictions.

5. Monitor, Evaluate, and Iterate: Continuously monitor and evaluate the performance of your analytics initiatives. Learn from the outcomes and iterate accordingly to refine your strategies over time.

Leveraging analytics to optimize your strategy can revolutionize your business operations. By harnessing the power of data, businesses can drive informed decision-making, improve efficiency, gain a competitive advantage, enhance personalization, and mitigate risks. While challenges such as data quality, resource constraints, scalability, and talent shortage exist, adhering to best practices can ensure successful implementation of analytics initiatives. Embrace the potential of analytics and empower your organization to make data-driven decisions that reshape the future.

Chapter 5: Establishing Your Affiliate Marketing Platform

Congratulations on reaching Chapter 5 of our comprehensive guide on affiliate marketing! By now, you should have a solid understanding of what affiliate marketing entails and why it is a legitimate and profitable business model. In this chapter, we will delve deeper into the practical aspects of setting up your affiliate marketing platform.

Building an effective affiliate marketing platform is crucial for your long-term success in this industry. A well-designed platform will not only attract potential customers but also provide a seamless experience for both affiliates and merchants. In this chapter, we will cover the various elements that contribute to a successful affiliate marketing platform and discuss how to optimize each one.

Choosing the Right Platform

When it comes to choosing an affiliate marketing platform, you have several options available. Some popular choices include affiliate networks, self-hosted platforms, and WordPress plugins. Each option has its own set of advantages and disadvantages, so let's explore them in detail.

1. Affiliate Networks: Affiliate networks act as intermediaries between affiliates and merchants. They provide a platform where affiliates can discover various products or services to promote and earn a commission on successful referrals. Some well-known affiliate networks include CJ Affiliate, ShareASale, and ClickBank. These networks typically handle all tracking, reporting, and payments, making them a convenient choice for beginners.

2. Self-Hosted Platforms: If you prefer more control over your affiliate marketing platform, consider setting up a self-hosted platform. This option allows you to customize your platform according to your specific needs. Popular self-hosted platforms include iDevAffiliate, Post Affiliate Pro, and HasOffers. While self-hosted platforms require more technical expertise, they offer greater flexibility and scalability.

3. WordPress Plugins: If you already have a WordPress website, you can leverage the power of plugins to transform it into an affiliate marketing platform. Plugins like AffiliateWP and WooCommerce can seamlessly integrate with your existing content management system, allowing you to manage affiliates, track referrals, and generate reports easily. WordPress plugins are an excellent choice if you want a cost-effective and user-friendly solution.

Designing Your Affiliate Marketing Platform

Once you've selected the right platform, it's time to focus on designing an aesthetically pleasing and user-friendly affiliate marketing platform. Remember, the first impression matters, and a poorly designed platform may discourage potential affiliates or customers from engaging with your offers. Here are some key design considerations to keep in mind:

1. Responsive Design: With the increasing usage of mobile devices, it's essential to ensure your platform is mobile-friendly and responsive. A responsive design adapts to different screen sizes, ensuring optimal viewing experiences across devices. This will enhance user engagement and improve conversion rates.

2. Intuitive Navigation: A well-structured and intuitive navigation system is crucial for guiding users through your platform. Ensure that your menu structure is straightforward, and important sections or pages are easily accessible. Additionally, use clear and descriptive labels to help visitors find what they're looking for quickly.

3. Visual Appeal: Use visually appealing elements, such as high-quality images, engaging videos, and eye-catching banners, to capture your audience's attention. A visually appealing platform not only creates a positive impression but also enhances the overall user experience.

4. Clear Call-to-Actions: To maximize conversions, make sure you have clear call-to-actions (CTAs) placed strategically throughout your platform. Use persuasive language and design elements to

create compelling CTAs that prompt visitors to take the desired action, whether it's signing up as an affiliate or making a purchase.

Setting up Affiliate Tracking and Reporting

Accurate tracking and reporting are the backbone of any successful affiliate marketing program. By implementing reliable tracking mechanisms, you can reward affiliates fairly and gain valuable insights into your campaign's performance. Here's what you need to consider when setting up affiliate tracking and reporting:

1. Cookie Tracking: Most affiliate platforms rely on cookies to track referrals accurately. A cookie is a small text file stored on a user's device when they visit your platform through an affiliate link. It helps attribute conversions to the correct affiliate and track performance metrics. Ensure that your platform uses secure and reliable cookie tracking to avoid any discrepancies or fraudulent activities.

2. Conversion Tracking: Implement a robust conversion tracking system to monitor sales, leads, or other desired actions. This system should accurately attribute conversions to the respective affiliates, allowing you to calculate commissions accurately. Explore different tracking options, such as pixel tracking or server-to-server tracking, to find the most suitable method for your platform.

3. Real-time Reporting: Timely and detailed reporting is crucial for

evaluating your affiliate marketing campaign's performance. Your platform should provide comprehensive reports on clicks, conversions, earnings, and other key metrics. Real-time reporting enables you to identify top-performing affiliates, optimize underperforming campaigns, and make data-driven decisions to improve overall results.

Commission and Payment Management

Establishing a fair and transparent commission structure is essential for maintaining strong relationships with your affiliates. While commission rates may vary depending on the industry and product type, it's important to strike a balance between profitability and attractiveness to affiliates. Consider the following factors when managing commissions and payments:

1. Competitive Commission Rates: Research the prevailing commission rates in your niche to understand what is considered fair and competitive. Offering attractive commission rates is a powerful incentive for affiliates to promote your products or services over competitors.

2. Multiple Payment Options: Provide a variety of payment options to accommodate affiliates from different regions or countries. Common payment methods include PayPal, direct bank transfers, or gift cards. Ensure that your payment process is secure, reliable, and hassle-free, promoting trust and loyalty among your affiliates.

3. Timely Payments: Promptly pay your affiliates according to the agreed upon payment schedule. Timely payments enhance your credibility and motivate affiliates to continue promoting your offers. Consider automating your payment process to ensure efficiency and reliability.

In this chapter, we covered the fundamentals of establishing your affiliate marketing platform. By carefully selecting the right platform, designing an appealing website, implementing effective tracking and reporting mechanisms, and managing commissions and payments, you can create a platform that attracts both affiliates and customers. Remember, a well-designed and functional platform is the launching pad for your success as an affiliate marketer. Now, let's move on to Chapter 6, where we'll explore strategies for driving targeted traffic to your affiliate offers.

Creating a Professional and Engaging Website or Blog

In today's digital age, having a professional and engaging website or blog is essential for individuals and businesses alike. Whether you are a freelancer, a small business owner, or simply someone who wants to share their thoughts and ideas with others, a well-designed online presence can help you reach a wider audience and establish credibility in your field. In this chapter, we will explore the key elements and best practices for creating a website or blog that captivates visitors and keeps them coming back for more.

1. Define Your Purpose and Target Audience

Before diving into the design and development process, it is crucial to determine the purpose of your website or blog and identify your target audience. Are you aiming to sell products or services, share valuable information, or connect with like-minded individuals? Understanding your goals will help you craft a clear message and design that resonates with your desired audience.

2. Choose a Memorable Domain Name

Your domain name is the web address that visitors will use to access your website or blog. It should be easy to remember, relevant to your content, and ideally, reflect your brand or personal identity. Consider using keywords related to your niche to improve search engine optimization (SEO) and increase your chances of being discovered by potential visitors.

3. Invest in Professional Web Design

While many platforms offer pre-designed templates, investing in professional web design can give your website or blog a unique and polished look. A professional designer will ensure that your site is user-friendly, visually appealing, and responsive across various devices. Remember, the first impression is critical, and a well-designed website speaks volumes about your professionalism and attention to detail.

4. Craft Compelling Content

Once your website or blog is visually appealing, it's time to focus on the core element that will keep visitors engaged: your content. Create high-quality, original content that demonstrates your expertise and provides value to your audience. Research your topic thoroughly, use credible sources, and write in a clear and engaging manner. Incorporate visuals such as images, infographics, or videos to enhance the overall user experience.

5. Optimize for Search Engines

To increase visibility and attract organic traffic, it is crucial to optimize your website or blog for search engines. Research relevant keywords related to your content and incorporate them strategically throughout your website, including in your titles, headings, meta descriptions, and image alt tags. Make sure your website's structure is logical and easy for search engine crawlers to navigate.

6. Focus on User Experience

A positive user experience is vital for any website or blog. Ensure that your navigation is intuitive, and important information is easily accessible. Minimize loading times by optimizing your images and code. Consider implementing interactive features, such as comment sections or forums, to encourage user engagement. Regularly update your content and ensure that it remains relevant and valuable to your audience.

7. Mobile Optimization is Essential

With an increasing number of people accessing the internet through mobile devices, it is vital to optimize your website or blog for mobile users. Responsive design ensures that your content is displayed correctly on various screen sizes and devices. Test your website or blog on different mobile devices to ensure a seamless mobile browsing experience for your visitors.

8. Incorporate Social Media Integration

Social media plays a significant role in today's digital landscape. Integrate social media icons and sharing buttons on your website or blog to encourage visitors to easily connect and share your content on their preferred platforms. Actively maintain social media profiles that complement your website or blog and use them to promote your content, interact with followers, and build a community around your brand or ideas.

9. Implement Analytical Tools

To understand your website's performance and track your progress, it is essential to implement analytical tools such as Google Analytics. These tools provide valuable insights such as the number of visitors, the most popular pages/posts, the average time spent on your site, and the referral sources. Use these insights to identify areas for improvement and to tailor your content to better meet your audience's needs and preferences.

10. Regularly Update and Maintain Your Website or Blog

Consistency is key when it comes to maintaining a professional and engaging website or blog. Regularly update your content to keep it fresh and relevant. Fix any broken links, update outdated information, and ensure that your website or blog is free from errors or glitches. Regularly back up your data to prevent loss and maintain site security.

Creating a professional and engaging website or blog requires careful planning, quality content, and continuous effort. By defining your purpose, understanding your target audience, and implementing best practices such as professional design, search engine optimization, and mobile optimization, you can establish a strong online presence that captivates and retains visitors. With consistent updates, regular maintenance, and integration of social media and analytical tools, you can build a loyal audience base and achieve your desired goals.

Search Engine Optimization (SEO) for Visibility and Traffic

In the vast and ever-evolving digital landscape, where millions of websites compete for attention, visibility and traffic have become crucial factors for online success. Whether you are an established business, a budding entrepreneur, or simply an individual looking to make your mark in the virtual realm, search engine optimization (SEO) is the key to unlocking the doors to increased visibility and enhanced traffic. This chapter will delve into the intricacies of SEO, exploring its various components, strategies, and best practices.

Understanding Search Engine Optimization

Search engine optimization is the process of enhancing a website's visibility and increasing organic traffic through various on-page and off-page optimizations. The ultimate goal is to rank higher in search engine results pages (SERPs) for relevant queries made by users. Since most online experiences begin with a search engine, appearing in the first few positions can significantly impact the amount of organic traffic a website receives.

SEO is a multidimensional discipline that encompasses several technical, creative, and analytical aspects. It requires a concerted effort to optimize various elements of a website, understand user behavior, and adapt to search engine algorithm updates. While SEO may seem intimidating, especially for newcomers, a systematic approach can make it more manageable and yield long-term results.

On-Page Optimization: Fine-Tuning Your Website

On-page optimization involves optimizing the content and structure of individual web pages to improve their visibility and relevance to search engines. This includes several key elements:

1. Keyword Research: Keywords are the foundation of SEO. Identifying relevant keywords and incorporating them strategically throughout your content allows search engines to understand the topic and relevance of your website. Utilize keyword research tools and consider factors such as search volume, competition, and user intent to target the right keywords.

2. Meta Tags: Meta titles and meta descriptions provide concise summaries of the content on a web page. These snippets of information appear in search engine results and play a crucial role in attracting users. Optimize meta tags by including relevant keywords and crafting compelling copy within specified character limits.

3. Heading Tags: Heading tags (H1, H2, H3, etc.) structure the content on a web page, making it easier for search engines and visitors to navigate. Incorporate target keywords in heading tags while maintaining a logical hierarchy.

4. Content Optimization: High-quality, informative, and engaging content not only attracts readers but also boosts your website's visibility. Optimize your content by ensuring it is easily readable, incorporating relevant keywords naturally, and providing comprehensive answers to user queries.

5. Image Optimization: Images are crucial components of web pages, enhancing visual appeal and user experience. Optimize images by reducing file sizes, adding descriptive alt text, and including relevant captions.

6. URL Structure: Ensure that your URLs are concise, descriptive, and include relevant keywords. A clean URL structure helps search engines and users understand the content of a web page at a glance.

7. Internal Linking: Create a network of internal links throughout your website to establish a logical hierarchy and help search engines understand the relationships between different pages. Linking relevant content also encourages deeper exploration by users.

Off-Page Optimization: Building Your Web Presence

Off-page optimization focuses on improving a website's visibility and authority beyond its immediate pages. This involves building a strong online presence through various strategies:

1. Link Building: Acquiring high-quality backlinks from reputable

websites is a crucial off-page optimization strategy. These backlinks act as votes of confidence and credibility in the eyes of search engines, indicating that your content is valuable and worthy of ranking higher. Develop link-building strategies such as guest blogging, outreach to influencers, and creating shareable content.

2. Social Media Engagement: Engaging with a targeted audience on social media platforms not only increases brand awareness but also generates referral traffic to your website. Focus on platforms relevant to your niche, share valuable content, and foster meaningful interactions to build a loyal following.

3. Online Directories and Citations: Listing your website on reputable online directories and submitting accurate and consistent citations (NAP: Name, Address, Phone Number) helps improve local visibility and credibility.

4. Influencer Marketing: Collaborating with influential individuals or thought leaders in your industry can extend your reach and attract valuable traffic. By tapping into their established audience, you can significantly increase your brand's visibility.

5. Online Public Relations: Engaging in online PR activities such as press releases, sponsorships, and partnerships can create valuable backlinks, enhance your brand's reputation, and attract organic traffic.

Technical Optimization: Ensuring Accessibility and Usability

Technical optimization focuses on improving the technical aspects of a website to enhance its accessibility and usability. These optimizations not only benefit users but also make it easier for search engines to crawl and index your web pages. Key aspects of technical SEO include:

1. Site Speed: Slow-loading websites negatively impact user experience, conversion rates, and search engine rankings. Optimize your website's speed by compressing images, minifying code, and leveraging caching techniques.

2. Mobile Optimization: With the majority of internet users accessing the web through mobile devices, ensuring your website is mobile-friendly has become imperative. Responsive design, fast-loading mobile pages, and intuitive navigation on small screens are essential for SEO success.

3. Site Structure: A well-organized, logically structured website makes it easier for users and search engines to navigate and understand your content. Create an intuitive hierarchy, utilize breadcrumbs, and implement XML sitemaps to aid crawling and indexing.

4. SSL Certificate: Implementing an SSL certificate adds a layer of security to your website and is considered a ranking factor by search

engines. This certificate encrypts user data, instilling trust and confidence in your visitors.

5. Structured Data Markup: Structured data markup, such as schema.org, helps search engines understand the context and meaning of your content. This can lead to rich snippets in search results, enhancing visibility and click-through rates.

Monitoring and Continuous Improvement

SEO is a continuous process that requires constant monitoring, evaluation, and adaptation. Regularly analyze your website's performance using tools like Google Analytics, Google Search Console, and third-party SEO software. Monitor keyword rankings, organic traffic, user behavior, bounce rates, and other metrics to identify areas for improvement.

Stay informed about search engine algorithm updates to adapt your strategies accordingly. Engage with the SEO community through forums, blogs, and conferences to keep up with the latest trends and best practices.

Remember, achieving and maintaining high visibility and traffic through SEO is a long-term commitment. It requires patience, dedication, and a continuous willingness to adapt and evolve alongside the ever-changing digital landscape.

Chapter 6: Maximizing Affiliate Earnings and Scaling Up

In the world of online marketing, affiliate marketing has emerged as a powerful way for individuals and businesses to generate passive income. The idea behind this strategy is simple yet effective— promote products or services of other companies and earn a commission for each sale made through your referral link. As lucrative as it sounds, affiliate marketing requires careful planning and execution to maximize earnings and scale up your business. In this chapter, we will delve into the various strategies and tactics that will help you boost your affiliate earnings and take your business to new heights.

Choosing Profitable Niches

One of the fundamental aspects of successful affiliate marketing is selecting profitable niches. A niche refers to a specific segment of a larger market. By focusing on a niche market, you can tap into a concentrated customer base and offer more targeted solutions. When choosing a niche, consider factors such as competition, demand, and profitability. Conduct thorough research to identify niches that have a sufficient customer base yet do not have overwhelming competition. Tools like Google Trends and keyword research tools can provide valuable insights on search volume and competition levels for different niches.

Building a Strong Affiliate Network

To maximize your earnings, it is crucial to build a strong affiliate network. The quality of your partners greatly influences your success in affiliate marketing. Seek out reputable companies with high-converting products or services that align with your niche. Look for affiliate programs that offer generous commissions, provide useful promotional materials, and have reliable tracking systems. Building relationships with industry leaders and influencers can also help you gain access to exclusive promotional opportunities and expand your affiliate network.

Creating High-Quality Content

Content plays a vital role in driving traffic to your affiliate offers and converting visitors into customers. To maximize your earnings, consistently create high-quality, valuable content that resonates with your target audience. This could include blog posts, videos, infographics, or product reviews. Optimize your content for relevant keywords and incorporate affiliate links seamlessly into your content. Avoid excessive promotion or overloading your content with affiliate links, as this can come across as spammy and drive away potential customers.

Utilizing Effective SEO Techniques

Search Engine Optimization (SEO) is critical to ensuring your affiliate website ranks high in search engine results pages (SERPs). By optimizing your website for relevant keywords, you can increase organic traffic and enhance your chances of making successful conversions. Perform keyword research to identify the most relevant keywords for your niche, and strategically incorporate these keywords into your website's content, meta tags, and URLs. Additionally, ensure your website is mobile-friendly, loads quickly, and provides a seamless user experience to improve your search engine rankings.

Leveraging Social Media Platforms

In today's digital age, social media platforms offer immense opportunities for affiliate marketers to reach and engage with their target audience. Utilize platforms such as Facebook, Instagram, Twitter, and LinkedIn to promote your affiliate offers and connect with potential customers. Use compelling visuals, catchy captions, and engaging content to attract and retain followers. Leverage social media advertising options to amplify your reach and target specific demographics that align with your niche. Regularly monitor and analyze your social media performance to refine your strategies and optimize your conversions.

Embracing Email Marketing

Email marketing remains one of the most effective ways to nurture leads and drive conversions. By building an email list of subscribers interested in your niche, you can establish trust, provide valuable content, and promote affiliate products or services. Create a compelling lead magnet, such as an ebook or exclusive content, to incentivize visitors to subscribe to your email list. Send regular newsletters, personalized promotions, and helpful tips to keep your subscribers engaged and interested in your recommendations. Be transparent about your affiliate relationships and only promote products or services that you genuinely believe in, as trust is essential in email marketing.

Analyzing Data and Optimizing Performance

To maximize your affiliate earnings, it is essential to track and analyze data regularly. Set up tracking systems and utilize analytics tools to monitor key performance indicators (KPIs) such as click-through rates, conversion rates, and revenue generated. Identify trends, patterns, and areas for improvement, and adjust your strategies accordingly. A/B testing, where you compare different variations of your content or promotional messages, can help you identify the most effective methods for driving conversions. Continuously optimize your campaigns based on data-driven insights to maximize your affiliate earnings.

Scaling Up Your Affiliate Business

Once you have established a profitable affiliate marketing system, it is time to scale up your business and enhance your earnings further. Consider expanding into new niches, diversifying your sources of traffic, or partnering with more affiliate programs. Continuously refine your strategies, invest in automation tools to streamline your processes, and consider outsourcing certain tasks to free up your time for strategic planning and growth. Collaborate with other affiliates or industry experts to create joint ventures or launch your own products or services. Scaling up requires ambition, resilience, and a willingness to adapt to changing market dynamics.

Maximizing affiliate earnings and scaling up your business require dedication, strategic planning, and continuous improvement. By selecting profitable niches, building a strong affiliate network, creating high-quality content, utilizing effective SEO techniques, leveraging social media platforms, embracing email marketing, analyzing data, and constantly refining your strategies, you can unlock the full potential of affiliate marketing. As you navigate the evolving landscape of online marketing, remember that success comes to those who are consistent, adaptable, and always ready to learn and grow.

Beyond Beginners: Scaling Your Affiliate Business

Congratulations! If you're reading this chapter, it means you've taken the initial steps to establish your affiliate business successfully. You've navigated the world of affiliate marketing, experimented with various marketing strategies, and started generating a steady stream of income. Now, it's time to take your business to the next level by scaling up and expanding your affiliate empire.

Scaling your affiliate business requires a strategic approach to maximize your revenue potential while maintaining the quality and integrity of your brand. In this chapter, we'll explore practical tips, techniques, and proven strategies to help you grow your affiliate business with sustainable success.

1. Diversify Your Affiliate Programs:
While getting comfortable with promoting a handful of affiliate programs is a key part of starting as a beginner, scaling your business requires diversification. Look for new affiliate programs and products within your niche, creating a diversified portfolio of partnerships that align with your audience's interests. This approach will not only expand your revenue streams but also safeguard your business against any unforeseen changes in a particular program or market.

Remember, quality trumps quantity when it comes to affiliate programs. Prioritize selecting reputable brands that offer competitive commissions, valuable products, and exceptional customer service. By expanding your network of affiliate partnerships, you'll be able to tap into new audiences and reach potential customers that were beyond your initial reach.

2. Optimize Your Content Strategy:

Scaling your affiliate business goes hand in hand with a robust content strategy. As you expand, ensure your content creation process aligns with your growing objectives. Invest in high-quality content, tailored to resonate with your target audience, and provide genuine value. Focus on creating informative blog posts, engaging videos, and eye-catching social media content that will captivate your audience and drive traffic to your affiliate links.

Additionally, devise an effective SEO strategy to improve your website's organic visibility. Conduct thorough keyword research, optimize your site's structure, and consistently publish keyword-rich, relevant content to boost your search engine rankings. This will attract more organic traffic and increase the potential for conversions.

Remember, quality content is king. Go beyond merely promoting products and focus on building trust and authority within your niche. The more valuable and insightful your content is, the more likely your audience will trust your recommendations and follow through with a purchase.

3. Leverage the Power of Email Marketing:

Email marketing remains one of the most effective ways to scale your affiliate business and build a loyal customer base. By collecting email addresses through lead generation strategies, such as offering exclusive content or valuable resources, you can nurture relationships with your audience and keep them engaged.

Craft compelling email sequences that provide subscribers with valuable content, product recommendations, and exclusive offers. Be careful not to overwhelm them with constant promotional emails – aim for a healthy balance between informative and promotional content. Nurture your subscribers, build trust, and establish a strong connection, so they remain receptive to your recommendations and become repeat customers.

4. Embrace Social Media for Promotion:

In the digital age, social media platforms are a powerful tool for scaling any online business. With billions of active users, platforms like Facebook, Instagram, Twitter, and YouTube offer endless opportunities to connect with your target audience. Formulate a robust social media strategy that incorporates engaging and visually appealing content to promote your affiliate products effectively.

Leverage the right mix of organic and paid social media campaigns to amplify your brand's reach. Engage with your followers, respond to comments and messages promptly, and actively participate in relevant communities or groups. Collaborate with influencers or thought leaders in your niche to widen your reach and establish your authority within the industry.

Remember, authenticity is crucial on social media. Avoid overtly salesy language or promoting products excessively. Instead, focus on building relationships, sharing valuable content, and subtly incorporating your affiliate promotions where appropriate.

5. Automate and Outsource to Streamline Processes:
As you scale your affiliate business, it becomes essential to automate and outsource certain tasks to streamline your processes. Utilize automation tools to schedule social media posts, manage email campaigns, and track your affiliate links' performance. This will free up your time, allowing you to focus on strategy and growth.

Consider outsourcing repetitive or time-consuming tasks like content creation, graphic design, or customer support to capable freelancers or agencies. Investing in professional support where needed will help you maintain the quality and efficiency of your operations as you expand.

6. Continuously Learn, Optimize, and Adapt:
The world of affiliate marketing is ever-evolving. To stay ahead and scale your business successfully, you must be open to continuous learning, optimization, and adaptation. Keep abreast of industry

trends, attend webinars or conferences, and read books or blogs by experts in the field.

Regularly analyze your data and metrics to identify what's working and what isn't. Experiment with different strategies, test new affiliate programs, and optimize your funnels to maximize your conversion rates. Be willing to adapt your approach based on the insights you gather, and always strive for improvement.

Remember, scaling your affiliate business requires patience, perseverance, and commitment. Set realistic goals, stay consistent, and don't be discouraged by setbacks. With the right strategies and an unwavering focus on your audience's needs, you can take your affiliate business beyond beginners and reach new heights of success.

This chapter has provided you with a roadmap to expand and scale your affiliate empire. Take these insights, implement them alongside your passion, and embark on this exciting phase of your affiliate marketing journey. Good luck!

Exploring Advanced Affiliate Marketing Techniques

Welcome to Chapter 6.2 of our comprehensive guide on affiliate marketing! In this chapter, we will delve into the world of advanced affiliate marketing techniques. Now that you are familiar with the basic concepts and strategies, it's time to take your affiliate marketing game to the next level. We will discuss six advanced techniques that will help you maximize your earnings and achieve exceptional success in the affiliate marketing industry. So, without further ado, let's dive into the exciting world of advanced affiliate marketing!

1. Relationship Building:

Affiliate marketing is not merely about promoting products; it's also about fostering strong and valuable relationships with both advertisers and your audience. Building and maintaining genuine relationships is vital for long-term success in this industry. Take the time to engage with your audience, respond to their queries, and provide valuable content that addresses their needs. Additionally, maintain open lines of communication with your advertisers to understand their goals, offers, and target audience better. By establishing strong relationships, you can gain insider knowledge about upcoming products, receive higher commission rates, and exclusively collaborate on promotional campaigns.

2. Niche Expansion:

If you have been successful in one particular niche, it's time to consider expanding your reach into different niches. Exploring new niches allows you to tap into different markets, diversify your income streams, and extend your influence. Conduct thorough research to identify emerging niches with untapped potential, analyze competition density, and assess profitability. Once you've chosen a new niche, leverage your existing expertise and adapt your strategies to suit the unique characteristics and preferences of the new target audience. Remember to stay true to your brand while exploring new niches, ensuring your audience can still see the value you offer.

3. Content Optimization:

To truly stand out in the crowded affiliate marketing space, it is essential to invest time in content optimization. Creating exceptional, high-quality content that provides immense value to your audience is crucial. Optimize your articles, blog posts, and other forms of content by incorporating relevant keywords, optimizing headings and subheadings, and organizing content in a visually appealing manner. Additionally, make your content shareable by integrating social media buttons, inviting readers to comment, and encouraging interaction. By optimizing your content, you maximize your visibility, attract more organic traffic, and increase your chances of converting visitors into customers.

4. Email Marketing Automation:

As an affiliate marketer, having an email list is an invaluable asset. However, manually managing email campaigns can be time-consuming and challenging. That's where email marketing automation comes to the rescue. By using reliable email marketing tools, such as MailChimp or ConvertKit, you can automate your email campaigns, saving time and effort. Segment your email list based on demographics, interests, and purchasing behaviors to deliver personalized content and offers to different segments. Implementing automation allows you to nurture leads, promote products, and build a strong relationship with your subscribers consistently.

5. Influencer Collaborations:

Influencer marketing has gained tremendous popularity in recent years, and integrating it into your affiliate marketing strategy can yield remarkable results. Collaborating with influencers allows you to tap into their massive, dedicated audience and gain instant credibility. Identify influencers in your niche who align with your brand values and have an engaged following. Approach them with a well-thought-out collaboration proposal offering mutual benefits. For instance, you could request them to review your affiliated products or have them share your content with their audience. Influencer collaborations open up new avenues for exposure, attracting quality leads and increasing your chances of conversion.

6. Data-Driven Decision Making:

The digital age provides us with an abundance of data. To gain a competitive edge in affiliate marketing, it's crucial to harness this data and use it to inform your decision-making process. Analyze your website's analytics to understand visitor behavior, traffic sources, and conversion rates. Identify which marketing channels are driving the most conversions and focus your efforts on optimizing those channels further. Utilizing A/B testing enables you to test different variations of your content, layouts, and calls to action, allowing you to make data-driven decisions. By consistently monitoring and adapting based on data insights, you can achieve significant growth and success as an affiliate marketer.

You have now explored advanced affiliate marketing techniques that are essential for success in this dynamic industry. From building valuable relationships, expanding into new niches, and optimizing your content to leveraging email marketing automation, influencer collaborations, and data-driven decision making, you have acquired valuable knowledge to propel your affiliate marketing efforts to the next level. Remember, mastering these advanced techniques requires dedication, persistence, and a willingness to adapt. So, stay committed, keep learning, and continue refining your strategies as you embark on your journey towards phenomenal affiliate marketing success!

Automated Tools and Their Role in Passive Income

Welcome to Chapter 6 of our book on passive income! In this chapter, we will delve into the exciting world of automated tools and discover how they play a significant role in creating and maintaining passive income streams. As technology advances, so does our ability to automate various aspects of our lives, including income generation. From intelligent software applications to online platforms, the opportunities to leverage automation for passive income are vast and ever-growing. Join us as we explore the different types of automated tools and how they can become valuable assets in your quest for financial freedom.

Section 1: Understanding Automated Tools

To truly grasp the potential of automated tools in passive income, we must first comprehend their fundamental concepts. Automated tools are any technological resources that assist in performing tasks or processes without requiring constant manual input. These tools can operate autonomously or with minimal human intervention, freeing up time and effort for other income-generating activities. By leveraging technological advancements, individuals can create scalable and sustainable income streams that generate revenue continuously, even when they are not actively engaged in the process.

Section 2: The World of Automated Trading

One of the most prominent sectors benefitting from automated tools is the financial market, particularly through the concept of automated trading. Automated trading refers to the use of algorithms and computer programs to execute trades automatically, based on predefined criteria and market conditions. With the help of advanced trading platforms, traders can develop trading strategies, set parameters, and let the system do the work. The allure of passive income in the form of automated trading lies in the potential to generate profits without the need for constant monitoring or active participation.

Section 3: Maximizing eCommerce Potential through Automation

Another thriving domain empowered by automated tools is eCommerce. Online marketplaces and platforms have revolutionized the way people buy and sell products, thereby creating a plethora of opportunities for passive income. Automated tools such as dropshipping solutions, inventory management systems, and digital marketing platforms streamline and simplify the eCommerce process. By integrating these tools into an eCommerce business model, entrepreneurs can leverage automation to generate revenue effortlessly, allowing for more time on strategy development or pursuing other ventures.

Section 4: The Power of Content Creation Automation

The rise of digital media has opened up countless possibilities for content creators to monetize their skills and expertise. However, creating quality content consistently can be time-consuming and challenging. This is where automated tools come to the rescue. AI-driven software can generate written articles, edit videos, create graphics, and even compose music. By automating parts of the content creation process, content creators can focus their efforts on developing unique ideas, connecting with their audience, and exploring additional monetization avenues, ultimately boosting their passive income potential.

Section 5: Leveraging Automation for Online Advertising

Online advertising is a crucial component of many businesses' revenue streams. From Google Ads to social media campaigns, businesses put substantial effort into reaching their target audience effectively. Automated tools enable marketers to streamline and optimize their advertising efforts, maximizing the return on investment while minimizing manual intervention. With the help of AI algorithms, these tools ensure that every advertising dollar spent is directed toward the most promising avenues, thus allowing marketers to enjoy a steady passive income stream from ad revenue.

Section 6: The Role of Automated Customer Relationship Management

Building and maintaining strong relationships with customers is vital for long-term success in any business. However, the task of managing customer relationships can be time-consuming and resource-intensive. Automated customer relationship management

(CRM) tools take on this responsibility, ensuring that customer interactions are handled efficiently and effectively. By automating routine tasks, such as lead nurturing, customer follow-ups, and feedback collection, businesses can free up valuable time to focus on growth and revenue-generation strategies, all while maintaining a positive passive income stream.

Section 7: Exploring the Potential of Robo-Advisors

Investing is a popular avenue for generating passive income, but it often requires knowledge, experience, and time commitments. Robo-advisors, automated investment platforms that rely on complex algorithms, have democratized investing by making it accessible to a broader audience. These tools provide personalized investment advice and execute trades on behalf of investors, based on their risk tolerance, financial goals, and market data. By automating the investment process, individuals can enjoy the benefits of passive income without having to develop expertise or spend countless hours managing their investment portfolio.

The Future Landscape of Affiliate Marketing

In recent years, affiliate marketing has experienced exponential growth, thanks to the rise of e-commerce and digital advertising. However, as with any industry, the landscape is constantly evolving, and affiliate marketers must adapt to stay ahead of the curve. In this chapter, we will explore the future of affiliate marketing and the key trends that will shape its landscape.

1. Artificial Intelligence (AI) Integration:
Artificial Intelligence technologies are transforming the way businesses operate, and affiliate marketing is no exception. AI integration allows marketers to analyze vast amounts of consumer data, identify potential affiliates more efficiently, personalize content, and improve conversion rates. AI-driven chatbots are also becoming more prevalent, providing instant customer support and improving user experiences.

2. Influencer Marketing Dominance:
Influencer marketing has become a dominant force in the digital space, with social media influencers playing a significant role in promoting products and driving sales. This trend will continue to strengthen as influencers develop more specialized niches and establish deeper connections with their audiences. Affiliate marketers will need to leverage influencer partnerships to enhance

their campaigns and reach a larger customer base effectively.

3. Increased Focus on Mobile:

The rapid growth of smartphone usage has shifted the digital landscape towards mobile platforms. It is projected that mobile commerce will account for over half of all e-commerce sales by 2021. As such, affiliate marketers must prioritize mobile optimization to ensure seamless user experiences, responsive designs, and mobile-friendly content. Additionally, mobile apps will play a crucial role in affiliate marketing, offering unique opportunities for targeted marketing campaigns.

4. Video Content as a Driving Force:

Video content has experienced tremendous popularity across various platforms, such as YouTube, Instagram Stories, and TikTok. The rise of short-form videos, live streams, and video ads has created new avenues for affiliate marketing. Marketers can leverage video content to showcase product reviews, demonstrations, and endorsements while incorporating affiliate links directly into the video description or in-video overlays.

5. Localization and Personalization:

Consumers increasingly expect personalized experiences, and affiliate marketing will need to adapt accordingly. Localization, targeting specific geographic areas, allows marketers to tailor their campaigns based on regional preferences and cultural nuances. By personalizing the content, including language, imagery, and product selection, affiliates can build stronger connections with their target audiences, thereby increasing engagement and conversions.

6. Rise of Niche Markets:

While broad-based affiliate marketing will continue to thrive, we can expect a surge in niche markets. With advancements in analytics and AI, affiliate marketers can identify untapped niche audiences and cater to their specific interests and needs. Niche marketing fosters higher engagement rates and encourages consumers to trust affiliates as authorities within their chosen niches.

7. Blockchain Revolution:

Blockchain technology holds immense potential for improving transparency and security within affiliate marketing. By utilizing smart contracts, blockchain can ensure fair and timely payments between advertisers and affiliates, eliminating the need for intermediaries. Additionally, blockchain can enhance measurement accuracy by providing verified data on clicks, conversions, and other key metrics, mitigating fraud and building trust within the industry.

8. Voice Search Optimization:

With the rapid adoption of voice assistants like Amazon's Alexa and Google Assistant, optimizing affiliate marketing campaigns for voice search is crucial. Marketers will need to consider long-tail keywords and natural language usage to tailor their content for voice search queries. As voice technology continues to improve, voice-activated affiliate marketing campaigns may become more common, presenting new challenges and opportunities.

9. GDPR and Privacy Concerns:

In an era where data breaches and privacy concerns dominate headlines, affiliate marketers must prioritize compliance with regulations like the General Data Protection Regulation (GDPR). Building trust with consumers by being transparent about data collection practices, obtaining explicit consent, and ensuring secure data storage will be essential. Additionally, marketers should explore innovative ways to deliver personalized content without compromising user privacy.

10. Enhanced Tracking and Attribution:

Advanced tracking technologies will play a crucial role in affiliate marketing's future landscape. With the rise of multi-device usage and cross-channel campaigns, accurately attributing conversions to specific affiliates can be challenging. In response, marketers will need to adopt sophisticated tracking tools and attribution models to ensure fair compensation and optimize campaign performance.

In summary, the future of affiliate marketing is ripe with opportunities, but marketers must embrace new technologies, adapt to evolving consumer behaviors, and prioritize transparency and personalization. By staying ahead of the trends highlighted in this chapter, affiliate marketers can navigate the changing landscape and create successful, impactful campaigns.

Chapter 7: Overcoming Challenges and Staying Resilient

Life is a rollercoaster ride filled with ups and downs, unexpected twists and turns, and challenges that test our resilience. In Chapter 7, we delve into the art of overcoming these challenges and developing the mental fortitude required to stay resilient in the face of adversity.

Understanding Challenges

Challenges come in various forms and sizes. They might be personal, professional, or a combination of both. It could be an unexpected loss, a financial setback, a major career setback, or a health crisis. Regardless of the nature of the challenge, what sets apart individuals who thrive from those who despair is their ability to overcome difficulties with resilience.

Embracing Resilience

Resilience is the ability to bounce back from setbacks, adapt to change, and emerge stronger from adversity. It is not a fixed characteristic but rather a skill that can be cultivated and honed over time. Resilient individuals view challenges as opportunities for growth, leaning into discomfort instead of shying away from it.

Developing a Growth Mindset

One of the key components of resilience is developing a growth mindset. This is the belief that challenges and setbacks are not indications of personal failures but rather opportunities for learning and growth. Those with a growth mindset understand that setbacks are temporary and that failure is merely a stepping stone towards success. They embrace challenges as chances to stretch their capabilities and expand their potential.

Learning from Failure

Failure is an inevitable part of life. It is how we respond to failure that defines us. Resilient individuals view failure as a valuable learning experience, examining the lessons they can extract from the situation. Learning from failure involves analyzing what went wrong, identifying areas for improvement, and using that knowledge to navigate future challenges more effectively.

Cultivating Emotional Intelligence

Emotional intelligence, or EQ, is the ability to understand and manage our emotions and those of others effectively. It plays a crucial role in building resilience as it enables us to navigate challenging situations with composure and empathy. By understanding our emotional triggers and developing coping strategies, we can maintain a balanced perspective even in times of hardship.

Building a Support Network

No individual can navigate life's challenges alone. Building a strong support network is fundamental to maintaining resilience. Such a network could include friends, family, mentors, and therapists – individuals who provide emotional support, offer guidance, and help us overcome obstacles. Through shared experiences and collective wisdom, a support network becomes a reliable source of encouragement and validation.

Developing Coping Strategies

Resilient individuals proactively develop coping strategies to handle stress and challenges. Coping mechanisms can take many forms, including exercise, meditation, journaling, or pursuing hobbies. Engaging in self-care activities helps us recharge, refocus, and gain perspective when faced with adversity. Regular practice strengthens our ability to bounce back and stay resilient in the face of future challenges.

Maintaining a Positive Mindset

A positive mindset is a powerful tool in overcoming challenges. Resilient individuals understand the importance of maintaining an optimistic outlook and reframing negative situations as opportunities for growth. Positivity fuels motivation, creativity, and problem-solving skills. Consequently, such individuals are more likely to find innovative ways to overcome obstacles and maintain their resilience throughout the journey.

Harnessing the Power of Reflection

Reflection is a critical practice in building resilience. By taking the time to look back on our experiences, we can extract valuable insights and identify patterns. Reflection allows us to learn from past challenges, celebrating our successes and identifying areas for improvement. Furthermore, it builds self-awareness, enabling us to better understand our strengths, weaknesses, and triggers, thus equipping us with the tools needed to overcome future challenges.

Seeking Professional Help

In some cases, the challenges we face may be overwhelming, and resilience alone may not be sufficient. During these times, seeking professional help is a sign of strength. Therapists and counselors provide a safe space to explore our emotions, gain perspective, and develop coping strategies. Professional guidance and support can be the catalyst needed to overcome even the toughest of challenges.

Common Pitfalls to Avoid in Affiliate Marketing

Affiliate marketing has become a popular avenue for individuals and businesses to generate income online. The concept is simple – as an affiliate marketer, you promote products or services and earn a commission for every sale or lead generated through your efforts. It's an attractive proposition, as it offers the potential to earn passive income and work remotely.

However, like any entrepreneurial venture, affiliate marketing comes with its own set of challenges and pitfalls. In this chapter, we will delve into the most common mistakes made by affiliate marketers and provide practical tips on how to avoid them. By learning from the experiences of others, you can set yourself up for success in the competitive world of affiliate marketing.

1. Lack of Research and Understanding

One of the biggest mistakes rookie affiliate marketers make is jumping into a niche without conducting proper research and gaining a deep understanding of the industry. Many believe that simply creating a website or blog and filling it with affiliate links will lead to instant success. However, this couldn't be further from the truth.

To build a successful affiliate marketing business, you must invest time in researching your chosen niche thoroughly. Understand who your target audience is, identify their pain points and needs, and find out what products or services would genuinely benefit them. This not only helps you select the right affiliate programs but also enables you to produce relevant and engaging content that resonates with your audience.

2. Promoting Too Many Products

One common trap that affiliate marketers fall into is promoting too many products at once. While it may seem logical to diversify your offerings to maximize your earning potential, this approach often leads to diluted efforts and ultimately results in lower conversions and revenues.

Instead, focus on promoting a handful of high-quality, relevant products or services that align with your audience's needs. By becoming an authority in a specific niche and promoting products that you genuinely believe in, you build trust with your audience, increasing the likelihood of their purchase.

Remember, it's better to have a handful of well-targeted campaigns that generate consistent revenue than a broad range of products that yield little to no results.

3. Ignoring Content Quality

Content is king in the world of affiliate marketing. Your success as an affiliate marketer depends on the quality and relevance of the content you produce. Unfortunately, many beginner affiliate marketers compromise on content quality, opting for quantity over substance.

It's crucial to produce high-quality, informative, and engaging content that provides value to your readers. Be creative in your content creation efforts – write comprehensive blog posts, produce instructional videos, conduct interviews with industry experts, or collaborate with guest authors. By offering unique and valuable content, you establish yourself as a trusted source of information, encouraging your readers to return and potentially make a purchase through your affiliate links.

4. Neglecting SEO and Traffic Generation

Generating targeted traffic to your affiliate marketing website or blog is essential for success. However, many affiliate marketers make the mistake of solely relying on social media or paid advertising for traffic generation, while neglecting the power of SEO (Search Engine Optimization).

Search engines like Google are a significant source of organic traffic, which can prove highly effective in generating conversions. Invest time in learning about SEO best practices, such as keyword research, on-page optimization, and link building. By optimizing your content for search engines, you increase your chances of ranking higher in search results, driving more targeted traffic to your site.

5. Overlooking the Importance of Email Marketing

Email marketing remains one of the most effective strategies for affiliate marketers to nurture relationships with their audience and increase conversions. Unfortunately, many novice affiliate marketers fail to recognize this and neglect to build an email list from the start.

Building an email list allows you to establish a direct line of communication with your audience, enabling you to promote products and services effectively. Offer valuable content, such as e-books or exclusive deals, in exchange for email addresses, and use email automation tools to send personalized and targeted emails that encourage engagement and foster trust.

6. Disregarding Transparency and Ethics

Maintaining transparency and ethical practices is vital for long-term success in affiliate marketing. Some affiliate marketers tend to conceal their affiliate links or promote products without genuine belief in their efficacy. Such practices can result in the loss of trust and credibility with your audience.

Instead, be transparent about the affiliate relationships you have with the products or services you promote. Clearly disclose when a link is an affiliate link and only promote products you genuinely believe in and have tried yourself. Honesty and integrity are essential in building strong relationships with your audience, fostering loyalty, and increasing conversions over time.

7. Failure to Test and Optimize

Affiliate marketing is an ever-evolving field, and success relies on continually testing and optimizing your strategies. Many affiliate marketers make the mistake of setting up campaigns and forgetting to track their performance or make necessary adjustments.

It's crucial to monitor and analyze your website's analytics, track your conversions, and test different marketing tactics. A/B testing your landing pages, experimenting with different call-to-actions, or tweaking your content can yield significant improvements in conversion rates and ultimately boost your affiliate income.

By avoiding these common pitfalls and implementing effective strategies, you can set yourself up for success in the world of affiliate marketing. Remember, patience, persistence, and a genuine desire to provide value to your audience are the key ingredients for long-term profitability in this dynamic industry.

Navigating Fluctuations in the Digital Market

In this fast-paced era dominated by technology, the digital market has become an essential facet of our lives. Businesses, both small and large, are increasingly relying on the digital space to reach and engage with customers. However, understanding and successfully navigating the fluctuations in the digital market is no easy task. In this chapter, we will explore the challenges and opportunities presented by the ever-changing digital landscape and discuss strategies to adapt and thrive amidst these fluctuations.

Understanding the Digital Market:

Before delving into the intricacies of navigating digital market fluctuations, it is crucial to grasp the underlying principles. The digital market encompasses all online platforms and channels where businesses interact with customers, including websites, social media, search engines, and mobile apps.

Despite its vast scope, the digital market boils down to one fundamental principle: capturing and retaining customer attention. Digital consumers are bombarded with an overwhelming amount of information and choices daily. Thus, businesses must employ strategies to stand out, resonate with the target audience, and drive conversion rates.

Challenges Presented by Digital Market Fluctuations:

Adapting to the ever-changing digital market landscape can be a daunting task. Here are some key challenges that businesses face:

1. Rapid Technological Advancements: The digital market is strongly influenced by advancements in technology. New platforms, devices, and algorithms continuously emerge, altering consumer behavior, preferences, and expectations. Staying updated on technological shifts is essential to maintain relevance.

2. Increased Competition: The digital space has lowered barriers to entry, resulting in increased competition. Businesses must continuously innovate and differentiate themselves to stay ahead in an overcrowded market.

3. Changing Consumer Behavior: Consumer behavior is evolving rapidly, influenced by factors such as social media trends, personalization, and convenience. Understanding the shifting preferences and adapting marketing strategies accordingly is key to success.

Adapting to Digital Market Fluctuations:

To navigate the fluctuations in the digital market successfully, businesses must embrace agility, innovation, and engagement. Here are some strategies to consider:

1. Continuous Learning: The digital market is ever-evolving, making

continuous learning a necessity. Businesses should invest in training their teams and staying updated on the latest trends, tools, and platforms. By fostering a culture of learning, organizations can proactively adapt to market changes.

2. Data-Driven Decision Making: Leveraging data analytics and market research enables businesses to understand consumer preferences and behavior. Analyzing data helps identify patterns, detect emerging trends, and make data-driven decisions. This approach minimizes risks and maximizes returns on marketing investments.

3. Personalization: In an era of information overload, personalized communication is indispensable. Tailoring marketing messages, content, and offerings to individual consumers enhances engagement and fosters a sense of connection. Personalization helps customers feel valued and understood, ultimately driving loyalty and conversion rates.

4. Omnichannel Approach: The digital market is characterized by a multitude of platforms and channels. Businesses must adopt an omnichannel approach, ensuring a consistent brand presence across various touchpoints. This strategy facilitates a seamless customer experience, where users can transition seamlessly between online and offline interactions.

5. Embracing Innovation: Businesses that thrive in the digital market

embrace innovation. Exploring emerging technologies, such as artificial intelligence, voice search, or virtual reality, can provide a competitive edge. Being open to experimentation and adapting quickly to new trends can help businesses stay ahead of the curve.

6. Building Relationships: Digital consumers crave connection and authenticity. Building meaningful relationships with customers through engaging content, social media interactions, and personalized experiences fosters trust and loyalty. Nurturing a strong community and brand advocates can amplify a business's reach and influence.

7. Agile Marketing: The digital market is characterized by rapid change, requiring businesses to embrace agility. Implementing agile marketing methodologies, such as agile scrum or sprint cycles, enables quick adaptation and iteration. Agile marketing ensures that strategies and campaigns can be adjusted swiftly in response to market dynamics.

Navigating fluctuations in the digital market is a constant challenge for businesses. However, by understanding the digital landscape, adapting to changes, and embracing innovative strategies, organizations can harness the power of the digital market to their advantage. Continuous learning, data-driven decision-making, personalization, an omnichannel approach, innovation, relationship-building, and agile marketing are vital elements for success. By staying attuned to market fluctuations and proactively adapting their strategies, businesses can thrive in the ever-changing digital marketplace.

Compliance, Ethics, and Longevity in Affiliate Marketing

In the ever-evolving world of affiliate marketing, staying compliant, ethical, and maintaining longevity are crucial factors for success. Affiliate marketers are constantly faced with the challenge of balancing their aspirations for profit with the need to abide by ethical standards and legal regulations. This chapter delves into the importance of compliance, ethics, and longevity in affiliate marketing, and provides insights on how to navigate this complex landscape.

Understanding Compliance in Affiliate Marketing

Compliance refers to the adherence to applicable laws, regulations, and industry standards in affiliate marketing practices. In recent years, regulatory bodies across the globe have increased their scrutiny of the affiliate marketing industry, imposing stricter guidelines and penalties. Therefore, it is imperative for affiliate marketers to familiarize themselves with the various compliance obligations.

First and foremost, it is essential to understand the implications of consumer protection laws, such as the Federal Trade Commission's (FTC) guidelines in the United States. The FTC requires affiliates to disclose their relationship with the promoted product or service clearly. Failure to provide accurate and conspicuous disclosures could lead to fines, legal troubles, and damage to an affiliate marketer's reputation.

Additionally, marketers should pay attention to the requirements set forth by advertising networks or platforms they work with. These platforms may have their own guidelines and policies that affiliates must adhere to. Violating these guidelines could result in suspension or termination of the affiliate's account, negatively impacting their business.

To ensure compliance, it is recommended to stay updated with relevant laws, regulations, industry best practices, and any changes in the guidelines of advertising platforms and networks. Affiliate marketers should also consider consulting legal professionals with expertise in advertising and marketing to minimize potential risks and ensure compliance.

Embracing Ethics in Affiliate Marketing

While compliance ensures adherence to legal requirements, ethics play a vital role in maintaining trust and building long-lasting relationships with consumers. Ethical affiliate marketing entails being transparent, honest, and responsible in all aspects of marketing practices.

Transparency is crucial in affiliate marketing, especially when it comes to disclosing financial relationships with merchants or advertisers. Clearly stating that an affiliate relationship exists can help build trust among potential customers and enhance the credibility of affiliate marketers. Well-placed disclosures not only demonstrate ethical conduct but also help avoid potential legal issues.

Responsible marketing practices are equally important. Promoting falsely exaggerated claims or misleading information can harm the reputation of both affiliates and the products they endorse. Affiliate marketers should ensure that their marketing efforts align with the values, quality, and reliability of the products or services they promote. By maintaining integrity in their marketing strategies, affiliates can gain the trust of their audience and establish themselves as reputable industry players.

Building Longevity in Affiliate Marketing

Longevity in affiliate marketing requires a sustainable and ethical business approach. By prioritizing compliance, ethics, and establishing a solid reputation, affiliate marketers can position themselves for long-term success.

One key aspect of sustainability is diversification. Relying solely on one merchant or niche can be risky, as shifts in market trends or changes in affiliate program policies can negatively impact revenue. Affiliate marketers should strive to diversify their portfolio by promoting products or services from various reputable merchants. This diversification enables them to adapt to changing market conditions and reduce their dependence on a single income source.

Another essential factor for longevity is establishing relationships built on trust and credibility. This involves cultivating positive relationships with merchants, customers, and other affiliates in the industry. By fostering collaboration and supporting fellow affiliates, marketers can build a network of like-minded professionals who can offer guidance, share insights, and potentially collaborate on future projects. These relationships can contribute to sustained growth and opportunities for long-term success.

Additionally, staying updated on emerging trends, technological advancements, and changes in consumer behavior is crucial for staying relevant in the rapidly evolving affiliate marketing landscape. Affiliate marketers must stay informed about changes in search engine algorithms, social media platforms, and digital marketing strategies to continuously adapt and optimize their marketing campaigns.

Compliance, ethics, and longevity are vital components of a successful affiliate marketing business. Affiliate marketers must prioritize compliance with applicable laws and regulations to avoid legal repercussions and protect their reputation. Ethical conduct builds trust among customers and allows for sustainable relationships with merchants and peers. Building longevity in affiliate marketing requires diversification, cultivating trust-based relationships, and staying informed about industry trends. By embracing these principles, affiliate marketers can navigate the ever-changing landscape of affiliate marketing and position themselves for long-term success.